COPPER
MOUNTAIN
BOOKS

ISBN:
Paperback   978-1-963781-03-8

Your School SUCKS

Why Schools Fail to Measure Up and What to Do About It

Nicole Alioto, Ph.D.

To Tom

and Vita

Contents

Introduction

*Almost half of students who start college
don't complete the degree or certificate.*[1]

Reading scores have barely improved in 30 years.[2]

THESE ARE JUST A COUPLE OF NATIONAL EDUCATION statistics that suck, and they lead people to think *your* school sucks. As a school leader, you're working hard to make progress in an ever-changing landscape that is full of people who don't see local successes when reading national headlines. Add misinformed, inaccurate, and anonymous social media comments about education into the equation and the negativity about schools spreads like wildfire, making it difficult to dispel.

In schools like yours, it's challenging to meet the diverse needs of the student population, grow innovative programs, and "move the needle" toward success when there is widespread negativity about education. When negativity is compounded by challenges like cost per pupil increases, tuition hikes, staffing shortages, declining enrollment, or unfunded mandates, it can be hard to focus on student success. Yet, it is hard to ask for more money from taxpayers or students, better funding from state and federal coffers, and community support if the public doesn't see clear evidence of success. Recruiting and retaining the best employees becomes more difficult when the institution can't show that its efforts pay off with strong student performance and a robust student experience. And why would someone move to a community for your local K12 experience or choose to attend a college in your area if they don't feel the education is providing a sound return on investment?

1   Emma Cohen, "High School Longitudinal Study of 2009 (HSLS:09): A First Look at the 2021 Postsecondary Enrollment, Completion, and Financial Aid Outcomes of Fall 2009 Ninth-Graders." National Center for Education Statistics (NCES) Home Page, April 8, 2024, https://nces.ed.gov/pubsearch/pubsinfo.asp?pubid=2024022.

2   National Center for Education Statistics, "Reading Performance." https://nces.ed.gov/programs/coe/indicator/cnb?tid=4.

Without evidence of positive results that everyone can feel proud of, many schools will continue to struggle. If you are the leader of an institution experiencing funding, staffing, enrollment, or performance woes, you know everyone is looking to you for guidance. And if you can't deliver the desired results, your school, community, and career could be at risk.

Leaders like you and your teams are working extremely hard, and with obstacles like the ones above, it's essential to use evidence and improve measurement practices to ensure that you are doing the *right* things to get the *best* results.

It seems with all of the data, assessments, and tools available, money and time spent, and hard work done by you and your staff, your school should be seeing significantly more success. But student outcomes are still falling short.

Where can you find answers?

Right here! I've been in the educational research space since 1999, when I formed an institutional research and planning office at a community college. My career path continued with program evaluation, assessment, analytics, and more planning as I moved from higher education to a K12 agency where I created an office for regional data analysis. That experience using evidence to drive school improvement led me to IBM, where I was able to show schools around the country how to better use analytics in decision-making. However, in that role, I couldn't provide the ongoing support school staff needed; I wanted to be their partner in the work. So I started Alla Breve Educational Consulting LLC[3] in 2017 and continue to assist K12 and higher education institutions in the best use of measurement practices to transform their schools.

In each role, I saw the massive amounts of data institutions generate about students and academic performance. It can get pretty overwhelming when you are buried in day-to-day matters that require your immediate attention. How do you decide what information should be prioritized in the quest for success with so much data?

3   *Alla Breve* is the musical term for cut time; the company saves institutions time and energy through getting focused and measuring effectively. Visit *www.allabreveconsulting.com* and sign up for our newsletter.

Your school has so much data already, and it generates more every second. I have seen the exponential growth of data generation in my lifetime, and it is mind-blowing. The volume of data created worldwide as of 2023 was 120 zettabytes (for reference, one zettabyte is equal to a *trillion* gigabytes).[4]

For context, your laptop computer might have 500 gigabytes (GB) of storage. In the mid-90s, my first "home computer" (as they were called back then) had a whole 1 GB. In the days before cell phones and streaming services, I wondered what I would do with all that space. Many software programs I used ran off disks; programs weren't installed and stored on a hard drive or server. That was just a few decades ago. Imagine a few decades from now!

To acknowledge the volumes of data available in education, terms like "data-driven decision-making" are often overused. If I say that at a meeting, I can expect teaching and administrative staff alike to roll their eyes and groan with boredom. Since there are so many data points generated every second, of course we are *all* using data to inform decisions, right? But are schools using the *right* data to make the *best* decisions?

Instead of just using data to make decisions, schools need to have *data-driven cultures* where using the right data becomes habitual, expected, and embraced. But *how* do you cultivate and reinforce a data-driven culture that leads to success when there are gaps in student learning, funding cuts, stressed-out staff, a community that needs to be connected, mountains of data, and no time left in the day?

With all of the challenges school leaders like you face—which I hear referred to as constantly "putting out fires"—it's difficult to be proactive in creating and sustaining a positive culture around data and continuous improvement. From my experience working with schools, we're not seeing the improvements in the educational outcomes we want because

---

4   Bigdata, "50+ Incredible Big Data Statistics for 2024: Facts, Market Size & Industry Growth," Big Data Analytics News, March 1, 2024, https://bigdataanalyticsnews.com/big-data-statistics/#:~:text=The%20global%20big%20data%20technology,13.6%25%20during%20the%20forecast%20period.

in most schools' cultures: 1) we are not clear what we mean by success in education, and 2) attitudes toward educational measurement are getting in the way.

Let's focus on that first point: lack of clarity about what success means in education. Recently, I attended a national conference for K12 school leaders, and many were discussing **a lack of consensus about what success meant** for their students. They said the school community wasn't talking about what success looks like often enough, and they weren't working together for a common purpose.

As they say in marketing, if you don't tell your story, someone else will. When there are competing definitions of success, the students get caught in the middle of programs, services, and efforts that might miss the mark. And that means time and money spent on the wrong things. Few schools can afford to waste resources moving in the wrong direction.

Imagine building a house with a team of people. You have tools, materials, and a limited amount of time to build it because people are waiting to move in. But you don't have blueprints or a picture of what the house will look like when it's done. It would be dangerous and wasteful to build a weak foundation or unstable structure. So, you wait until the plans are finalized and the house can be envisioned by all. Why don't we do this in education when we have limited time or resources and lack the blueprint?

It seems wasteful and reckless in the context of home building, yet schools implement actions without the proper foundation far too often. You might have your materials and team but no clear picture of the expected result, or you might have the vision but no shared blueprints. In this book, I'll be your architect and help you get clear on your construction.

Second, measurement in education is often equated with large-scale testing (which is a Pandora's Box that we won't take on here). And review of data often becomes an item on an agenda or professional development day that staff members feel is a waste of time. Over and over, I've seen **negative perceptions like these influence educators' interest in using data effectively**. When there is little interest, little is accomplished.

Let's talk about building that house again. If members of the crew weren't trained in how to use the tools, would you want them working on the house? What if some of them just wanted to decorate the house and not build it? What if everyone wanted to use a hammer or screwdriver instead of power tools because they were less intimidating, but also less effective? With these attitudes at the work site, it will be difficult—if not impossible—to get the job done. We can see similar scenarios in schools when there is a lack of training, lack of interest, or lack of confidence in the effective use of evidence to support school improvement. Your job is to ensure your team is prepared, productive, empowered, and motivated. This book will help with that!

You may have experienced defense mechanisms from educators, used as a mask for the stress or negative attitudes they have about all things data. I know I see it in schools! Not everyone needs to be a data cheerleader; however, the practices around effective use of evidence to support learning still takes a back seat when there are interruptions throughout the process. Your role as a school leader is to keep the momentum around evidence-based decisions, even when there are distractions and negativity along the way.

Getting clear on your direction and ensuring that the best evidence-based practices are implemented will set up your school for success. I know this since I've spent the last 25 years working with institutions like yours and leaders like you solving this exact problem. I mentioned my career path earlier, but my research experience dates back even further. As a social psychologist, I focused on attitude and behavior change in a variety of settings, exploring how mindsets and situations influence actions. As a student who always loved school, I applied these skills in the education industry. Being able to use solid theoretical frameworks and measurement principles in schools meant my approach to data was different. Using data wasn't intended to check a box, it was to change behaviors and get schools to achieve their desired outcomes.

And, unlike many people, I have loved data and counting since I could remember. Ever since I was a little girl, I've counted to relax. Yes, *relax*. Whether in a waiting room wondering what the doctors might say or sitting in a classroom not knowing anyone at the start of the school year, I could *always* find something to count—windows, outlets, things that are blue.

As a primary school-age girl, I recall visiting the vocational school where my father taught, getting my hair washed by beautiful strangers, and counting the ceiling tiles because I was in a place with so many new, unfamiliar people. When I got a little older, I would use multiplication instead of addition to count more tiles.

In junior high school, the cross country coach recognized my athletic limitations in seventh grade (as the team waited for me to cross the finish line so everyone could go home) and moved me into the team statistician role in eighth grade. That was my first job in analytics! Even today, I notice when I am feeling some stress or discomfort, I seek out something to count. Like when I'm attending a funeral, I count the number of pews.

My love of math led me to a career of using data to help improve performance in our educational systems. From institutional research to program evaluation, and predictive analytics to strategic planning, I've supported K12 and higher education institutions in the effective use of data. As a researcher in the field of education, I focus on collecting the right evidence, using the most appropriate techniques, and making accurate decisions.

However, throughout my career, I've witnessed the stress that "doing data" has placed on staff and students. I have seen good data go bad in the wrong hands or when politicized in the name of student achievement. It actually hurts my heart to see people struggling so much with measurement and analysis, so I've dedicated my career to helping schools transform data into direction and do a better job of reaching their goals.

I've worked with leaders who struggle with creating a data culture, so if you aren't a "data person," this book is for you. Even if you think of yourself as a data-driven leader, this book will help uncover hidden roadblocks that are limiting your efforts to use evidence effectively.

Over the decades and into the present day, I hear the same pitfalls and problems regarding data, measurement, and school success. And that's why I wrote this book: to ensure school leaders get clear on what success means so they can measure what matters and achieve desired outcomes. I wrote this book to shine a light on the obstacles related to measurement that prevent school decision-making teams from realizing the results they seek. I wrote it to help change the way we think about using data in schools. You will probably recognize many of the examples in your own institution at some point. Being able to recognize the obstacles and the reasons behind them is the first part of the book.

Then in the second part, we highlight an approach to building a culture of evidence-based decision-making that ensures your institution moves in the right direction as a community.

Finally, we share a case study that shows what the steps look like when they are put into practice along with amazing results!

What this book does *not* include is a statistical training program or lessons in psychometrics. You're welcome.

This book is made for school leaders and education champions who want to know how to lead their school community, make the best decisions, and achieve more success. You don't have to be a data devotee, and you don't need the title of College President or School Superintendent to benefit from this book; you only have to be a person who is passionate about educational transformation and doing better for students. So are you up for the challenge of improving your school and making sure others know your school doesn't suck?

With activities that I've used to help schools overcome obstacles around data and insights from some of my favorite education, psychology, and business resources, you will be in a better position to accomplish your mission. By changing the way your teams function and changing the way you approach measuring success for your students, you will be changing lives in your community for the better *for years to come.*

Now let's get started.

DATA ARE

You will likely notice that the word "data" is treated as plural throughout the book. I am a purist: data *are*, datum or dataset *is*. Similarly, curricula are and curriculum is, alumni are and alumnus is, etc.

It is what it is: data are what they are.

PART 1

Why Schools Fail to Meet Their Goals

$$T = X + E$$

When reviewing classroom assessments, a teacher might notice that a test score doesn't seem to reflect a student's ability. When collecting survey results, you might notice perceptions seem very different from what you expected to find. These scenarios happen in education often, and they are usually the result of some kind of error getting in the way of learning the truth.

The formula above summarizes these examples and is at the core of measurement. The true situation (T) consists of what you measure (X) about the situation plus error (E) that gets in the way of seeing the truth. In the classroom example, maybe the student was hungry and didn't pay close attention to the questions; that is one kind of error getting in the way of showing true ability. Another would be that the questions asked were all multi-part prompts that required high levels of reading comprehension to show knowledge of the content; that could lead to more error. The more E we have, the more we have trouble seeing the true situation and making the best decisions. And worse, it could lead to making the *wrong* decisions.

In the first part of this book, we'll explore the common reasons why schools continue to fall short of reaching their goals. Whether it is looking at the wrong data, being unclear about what success is, interpreting data incorrectly, or just being sick of data, your school community faces obstacles that bring error into your work. The more obstacles there are, the less your school will be able to measure success accurately and accomplish its goals.

As you read through this section, how many of these obstacles do you encounter on a regular basis? At the end of each chapter in Part I, you'll have a chance to reflect on your school's situation and your experiences. Be sure to complete the reflection checklists as they will prepare you for Part II.

CHAPTER 1

Easy vs. Effective

*Nothing in the world is worth having or worth doing
unless it means effort, pain, difficulty...
I have never in my life envied a human being who led
an easy life. I have envied a great many people who led
difficult lives and led them well.*
—THEODORE ROOSEVELT

IF I PUT TEN MISSION STATEMENTS FROM TEN SCHOOLS on the table and shuffled them up, I would bet that those school leaders might be confused about which one was from their own institution. Most schools have similar goals and missions; they all use broad language and the latest buzzwords. According to a conversation I had with ChatGPT, the top themes that emerged for school district mission statements were the following:

1. *Student-Centered Learning,*
2. *Equity and Inclusion,*
3. *Community Engagement and Partnership,*
4. *Excellence in Education, and*
5. *Preparation for the Future.*

Would any educator disagree with these as the core elements within a mission statement? How many of these exist in your institution's mission statement? The difficulty is the next step: *putting the mission into action.*

With topics like "student-centered learning" and "excellence in education" within most missions, why isn't every school meeting its goals for student success? One main reason that many schools struggle is because *they aren't actually measuring the things they say they want to achieve.* With overly general terms in the mission, the school states a commitment to things like excellence or preparation. But without a clear idea of what those terms mean, there is no way to link actions and data to goals and missions. It can be an overwhelming task to make connections between strategies and evidence after programs are underway, so the easiest approach is to only look at the data you have readily available.

However, easy doesn't always mean effective.

To paraphrase Teddy Roosevelt's famous quote, anything worth doing requires an effort. And it is probably not going to be the easy route. In this chapter, we will take a closer look at three ways schools focus on the easy over the effective.

First, it is easier to count "things" than it is to measure the impact. When you start a wellness program, it's easy to count the steps you take every day, but it's harder to measure the impact of the activity, such as walking to increase your sense of wellness. Are 10,000 steps enough? Does walking make you feel better and improve your overall health?

When schools are looking to measure the impact of their programs, systems are usually in place to collect the "easy" data, but not the impact data. For example, I've seen schools spend thousands of dollars on assembly speakers on topics from inclusivity to career planning. These assemblies are usually required, so, of course, attendance is high. However, when I ask what difference the assembly made, there is a lack of response due to the lack of evidence. Post-assembly exit tickets or surveys would gauge immediate impact and a follow-up in four to six weeks after the event can determine if the content really changed attitudes or behaviors. Taking attendance was easy; measuring the impact requires more effort.

Second, it's easier to use your own ideas than it is to come to consensus. Have you watched any YouTube videos from wellness gurus? They have a lot of ideas, but imagine the impact it would have on true behavior change if they all came to a consensus about what works. Getting your team on the same page about what is most important won't be easy; however, it is necessary. You'll need to be prepared with the time, energy, and perhaps conflict resolution skills needed to build a consensus.

There has been more than one occasion when a school leader warned me before a meeting that the group has very different perspectives. Engaging groups like this in productive conversations can definitely challenge even the most skilled facilitator. It usually feels like herding cats. When I am in this kind of environment, I need the attendees to have a shared objective so we can stay on track. It isn't always easy to get to a consensus, but it is necessary if we want to accomplish anything.

Third, it's easier to be reactive rather than proactive. That is, it is easier to respond to a request or requirement rather than taking initiative without the pressure. Let me ask: have you ever cheated your step counter? If your hands move around without actually walking, it could count those hand gestures as steps. I've seen people do this when they have to share their results with others. They are trying to hit the number before their accountability check-in. That won't help them achieve their desired wellness goals, but it will get the wellness police off their backs for another week.

In education, if actions are done in order to check a box for accountability or some other requirement, then it's less likely that the school is going to accomplish its goals for student success. I watched schools chase state testing accountability targets for years. The staff would try to game the system by having students practice the most common items found on the test. Over the years, the school hit accountability targets, but the students never really gained the knowledge or skills to be prepared for their future.

The more of these "easy" activities you participate in, the more errors you add to your school's equation, making it harder to reach your institutional goals. When we measure the wrong things because it is easy or because we haven't clarified what the right measures are, then we will never do the right things to ensure lasting change. Let's reduce the decisional error and focus on what's effective in addition to what's easy.

Outputs and Outcomes

I can't count the number of times I have discussed this topic. If I did, it would be an *output*.

- "Outputs" refer to the tangible "countables" of your action plans. I call them the "whats" in the plan.
- "Outcomes" refer to the impact of the actions. I call them the "so whats."

Why does it matter which we collect? Do we actually need both?

Let's think about getting healthy again. There are a lot of activities you add to your life to become a better version of yourself. Things like taking 10,000 steps, drinking 64 ounces of water, monitoring your weight or protein or whatever: these are all *outputs*.

If I do all of those things, *so what*? Will I be healthier?

We need different measures to determine that, such as being taken off of blood pressure medicine, being able to keep up with the toddlers, or being able to pick out anything from a clothing retailer and knowing it will fit. These are *outcomes*.

If we do the things and hit the targets we set for our output measures, we *think* we will be healthier. We only *know* it by measuring outcomes, too. And what if after improving our output measures, we still have to take meds or can't catch up with the kiddos? Our output measures may not be the right information to improve our health goals. So we need to change our plan and track new output data, perhaps in addition to the existing data.

Before you run over to the treadmill, how does this apply to education?

Let's use something like engagement. Schools are looking to increase engagement through a variety of activities and/or communications. In this example, engagement is the *so what* of the activity. However, it isn't so clear how to measure that, so schools choose an easier option: participation, i.e., attendance.

Attendance is a "what" related to the activities. How many people showed up? Just because people showed up, does it mean they were engaged? Anyone who has a teenager knows the answer to this question!

It is important to measure attendance or participation because you can't be engaged if you haven't been exposed to the activity. *But…*you can't measure engagement just by counting bodies through the door. You need an engagement measure. And that requires defining what engagement is (which we will do in Part II of the book).

Here's another example: think about the teaching of new instructional approaches to literacy and the learning of literacy skills. The whole point of the new instructional approaches is to improve skills and foster the love of reading. Can you measure those things if the program was never taught?

First, you want to know if the program was taught as intended and perhaps even how many minutes a day. You'll also want to know which students participated in the new program in its entirety versus partially versus not at all. These counting activities are *output* measures. If you can check a box, it is probably an output measure. If you can get a total number of something, it is probably an output measure.

Now, after you've collected information about who received the instruction and how much of the new program was provided, so what? Did it make a difference? For this answer, we need to turn to measures of improvement in literacy skills. It might also be necessary to do an exit ticket or some type of thumbs up/thumbs down activity to get feedback from the students about their interest in the program, or in reading (in general).

Why is the distinction between outputs and outcomes important?

As an institution implements a program or strategy, it's critical to measure progress and assess impact by tracking results—*outputs* and *outcomes*. As you engage with others on the measurement of program impact, outputs are necessary but not sufficient on their own. You'll likely use output measures to ensure a strategy was actually implemented (as intended); however, to make the difference you want, it's necessary to measure outcomes, as those show progress towards the goals. Outcomes might be harder to collect, but if you can define it, you can measure it.[5]

To sum up this section, just because you hit your step count doesn't mean you're healthier, and just because you taught it doesn't mean they learned it. Outputs are important; outcomes are critical.

Different Perspectives

You have seen optical illusions that can be interpreted in more than one way. The image below depicts the "Rubin's Vase" illusion where some can see the vase first and some see the faces first. Which did *you* see first?

---

5   You could jump ahead to Part II if you can't wait to start clarifying your constructs!

If we aren't sure what we are supposed to be looking at, we might see different things, and we can both be right to an extent.

In education, there are many pieces of information at our fingertips. But what if everyone focused on different data points based on individual perspectives? Can your school make the desired progress if everyone is looking at the situation differently?

English Benchmark	Math Benchmark	Math Placement	Reading Placement	Writing Placement	Persist	Fall GPA
Advanced	Proficient	423	301	231	No	3.00
Basic	Below Basic	347	307	211	No	3.33
Advanced	Basic	393	304	266	Yes	3.66
Below Basic	Proficient	279	300	274	Yes	3.38
Proficient	Below Basic	318	300	321	No	3.03
Below Basic	Below Basic	269	303	353	Yes	3.40
Below Basic	Below Basic	221	304	335	No	3.43
Below Basic	Below Basic	272	307	336	No	3.08
Basic	Proficient	257	267	241	No	1.73
Below Basic	Below Basic	284	255	253	No	3.80
Basic	Below Basic	258	269	257	No	2.78
Below Basic	Below Basic	220	241	262	No	3.35
Below Basic	Below Basic	264	272	246	No	3.33
Proficient	Basic	282	257	244	No	3.13
Basic	Basic	265	247	271	Yes	3.28
Below Basic	Below Basic	283	267	295	Yes	3.35
Below Basic	Below Basic	321	282	239	No	3.35
Basic	Advanced	237	274	257	No	2.98
Basic	Proficient	285	295	258	No	3.03

Table 1: Sample Dataset from Sample School

Here is an example of a dataset from a sample school. In each column, there's an important indicator about students. We see a variety of results from English and math assessments, fall semester grade point average (GPA), and a persistence measure—that is, whether or not the student enrolled in the next semester.

Where in this dataset is "success"?

I might think the most important metric is GPA, and someone else might think it is proficiency levels, and you might think it's something that's not even there! If educators can't agree about what matters most for students, how can progress be made toward desired outcomes?

In the last section we talked about including output and outcome measures to determine success and used the example of engagement and wellness as outcomes that would need to be defined and measured. But how does an institution determine that engagement *is* what matters? And how do they determine what factor(s) will impact engagement the most?

Let's consider an example using an outcome related to achievement of basic skills. In elementary schools across the United States, there's a desire to have students read at grade level by the end of third grade. For students who aren't meeting that outcome, what should teachers look for as the most important indicator? Some would argue it's exposure to reading materials in the preschool years, others would look to phonemic awareness, while others would stress reading comprehension skills. Indeed, they all are right in some contexts, but which is the one to watch for *your* students? You probably track them all, but how do you know which matters most?[6] If one teacher is working on reading comprehension and another doesn't do anything extra to support literacy skills because "it's the parents' fault" the child can't read, then your school will be an inconsistent mess that confuses children and families. Inconsistency (a.k.a. lack of reliability in measurement language) is another form of error. And we don't want it.

6   While not the focus of this book, I have conducted predictive analytics projects looking at this very issue, and I suggest your school should do the same to determine which predictors (individually and in relation to others) are the most significant, historically, in your student population. Don't assume someone else's research will apply to your students if the sample in the study isn't representative of your students and your school configuration.

School teams need to come to consensus about what success means first in order to figure out what measures matter. Even if there are different perspectives at the start of the conversation, decision-makers need to identify the *most important* factors for success. They might be based on research, past practices, stakeholder perceptions, or all of the above. In Part II, we will explore the idea of key performance indicators and how they help schools stay on track.

In sum, it's easy to "agree to disagree" about different perspectives on optical illusions, but if members of your team can't get on the same page about student success, their efforts will be disjointed and ineffective—*and results won't measure up.*

Accountability to Whom and for What?

It is much easier to answer a question than it is to form a good one. Similarly, it can be easier to comply with a request from an external agency rather than meet a set of internally developed standards. Think about it: if the doctor says, "cut the salt," it's easier than coming to that conclusion on your own and then being self-motivated to cut it out.

There are a lot of local, state, federal, and international ranking and accountability systems asking you to report on a variety of things. The indicators they want to see aren't always aligned to *your* institutional mission. Since the data sent to external groups may be published widely or shared with non-educators (e.g., the local realtor using school data to sell houses), these indicators might seem a good place to focus energy—but are they really? Are these data really representative of what is working well for your students and what is not?

If these measures were the true indicators of success, then every school would develop plans based on those results, make some changes, and things would look better pretty quickly. I'd imagine it would be an issue for realtors with so many high-performing schools to choose from! So why is it that with all of this information required by accountability systems or published for all to see and judge in their local newspaper or community page on social media, schools aren't meeting all of their educational objectives? From what I've seen in my decades of interpreting data for school transformation, it's because these mandated external standards are generally not sufficient to drive true change.

Let's use an example of ranking systems. I've worked in places where there was interest in regional comparison data. Perhaps an institution sees it is in the top three for the dozens of schools in the area. Sounds pretty good, right?

Well, what if the percentage of students who achieved proficiency (the desired outcome) was 55%? Was that good enough based on the data they had available for their students? Was it good enough for the staff or for businesses looking to hire these students or families?

I shared with this particular institution that while their result was near the top of the list, it was like having the highest F in the class.

Instead of looking at the list, the school needed to determine if that was a good result based on what they knew about their students. Was this better, the same, or worse? What do other data about these students suggest? What was the target result the district was aiming for? The conversation should take these questions into account and create a plan to move students from that result to the desired outcomes, regardless of where the school landed on the regional list.

So, are our schools failing if they don't meet a standard that is not even appropriate for their goals?

It is easy to rely on these external agencies to dictate what schools should be focusing on. But remember, those education "authorities," like doctors, are busy; they collect the minimum and move on to the next case. They don't know you like you know you. The information they exclude is also error. You have more evidence about how your school works and what your constituents need than what the external agencies considered. You can be proactive. You can do better.

Reflection

So far we have been talking about better measures of success from the standpoint that schools need to look at how success is defined and measured. School teams may be tempted to track and analyze what is easy rather than what is important or truly making a difference, and they could be distracted from their mission by pressures to compare their institution to external standards. As this chapter revealed, it is easy to measure the wrong thing or use the wrong approach. But even if your school works hard to measure the right things, teams don't always take appropriate action. In the next chapter, we'll talk about why that happens.

Before moving on, what are the issues that prevent *your* institution from using data effectively and achieving desired outcomes?

How many of these have you experienced at your institution?

☐ Outdated and/or extremely general mission statement
☐ Focus on outputs over outcomes
☐ Lack of agreement about what success indicators are
☐ Pressure to meet external accountability standards

CHAPTER 2

How Good Data Can Go Bad

"When things go wrong, don't go with them."
ELVIS PRESLEY

IN THE LAST CHAPTER, WE TALKED ABOUT HOW THE LACK of a clear and shared definition of success can lead to collecting what is easy to measure rather than what is effective for making accurate decisions. Having people on your team looking at data from different perspectives or feeling pressure to meet external standards could lead to shortcuts in the review of evidence and increase the error in your judgments. With these approaches, schools are looking at the wrong things. And even when you are looking at the *right* things, there are still challenges that bring error into decision-making.

Think about the start of the school year: everyone is busy; the race is underway. As you speed around that racetrack, the faces in the crowd are a blur, the other cars in the race are trying to keep up, and on occasion, you check in with the pit crew to keep things running. When your workday is focused on getting you around that track, there is limited time to pause and reflect, so good information could be ignored. When there are too few in your pit crew, everyone has to take on multiple roles and responsibilities. And if someone in your crew takes on a new role but lacks the skills needed to perform tasks, even the best tools may not be used properly.

How many of these sound familiar?

There are a number of ways that good data can go bad, and I've worked with schools that had some or all of these issues going on.

Limited resources (like lack of time), limited skills from those taking on new roles, or even limited interest in the work needing to be done can detour data usage. If you want to be a transformational school leader, listen to Elvis: when good things go wrong, don't go with them. In this chapter, we'll explore each of these issues so you can recognize problems early and ensure good data become good information that will lead to the best decisions.

Problem 1: The assessment (measurement) process is time-consuming/labor-intensive.

If something takes a long time to do to get to the results, how excited are you to do it? Losing weight (and keeping it off) is a long journey, which is part of the reason it's so hard to do. And there is a reason why short videos are dominating our social media feeds: no one wants to watch a long how-to video or full-length interview to get to the three tips they need. In education, quality assessments take time to create, administer, and evaluate. The time it takes can make it a chore that nobody looks forward to.

An institution I worked with informed me that it takes the staff an entire week to administer a benchmark assessment, and they give the assessment three times a year. That's 15 days of testing (not counting additional days if a child needs extended time or a make-up test) that should lead to changes in the classroom. After each testing window, there is additional time needed to review the results, plan for changes to instruction or supports, and then implement those strategies.

With at least 15 days eating away approximately 10% of the instructional time, teachers didn't want to add *more* time out of the class, so the data weren't used to drive instruction. Instead, they only reviewed a building-level snapshot of student performance that didn't address individual student needs.

Think about the impact of all that testing time on the students. They focused mental energy and multiple days taking an assessment with nothing changing as a result. Class continued as usual. It surely seemed like a waste of time (because it was), and they likely won't try too hard on future assessments. Would you want to do anything for weeks at a time and not know if you did it right or how you could have done it better?

There are dozens of studies connecting teacher feedback with student engagement and motivation. The Association for Supervision and Curriculum Development shared a post from Jane Pollock, which stated:

> *"As students receive more feedback and thus become more engaged in learning activities, their actions and self-assessments provide more feedback to teachers, who, in turn, make better decisions about instruction."* [7]

Unfortunately, I've seen many schools over-testing and under-assessing. With so much time in testing situations,[8] it is hard to make time to organize and analyze the data and review the results, and also make changes before students get another required assessment. It is important to ask: which assessments are actually useful for improving student learning outcomes? How many assessments are given in the same week across subjects? Is the amount of time to administer an assessment proportionate to the amount of use?

When schools spend time on the wrong testing and assessment practices, they lose the opportunity to collect and use good evidence to support learning. Consider how your teaching staff is assessing, *and also* how they are using results to inform instructional practices and engage students in their learning.

---

7   Pollock, Jane E. "How Feedback Leads to Engagement." ASCD, September 1, 2012. https://www.ascd.org/el/articles/how-feedback-leads-to-engagement.

8   And let's add in frequent homework that is assigned and graded without constructive feedback

Problem 2: The assessment (measurement) skills of staff are not developed in education training programs.

Not all education degree programs require future teachers to learn assessment and measurement to the degree that they should. They get a lot of preparation on the teaching side, but not the same amount of instruction on the learning side. When this pair is out of balance, it will set up the school community—staff and students—for failure and disappointment.

The first time a student came into my office hours in tears still sticks in my mind over 25 years after the fact. Some faculty like making students cry. I am not one of them. When I taught psychometrics[9] at the undergraduate level, a student entered my office, eyes welling up. She was struggling with the concepts and didn't understand most of the class. She asked a lot of questions about basic statistics that were needed to understand the more complex topics contained in the course. It turns out, the institution required psychology students to have statistics as a prerequisite to the course I was teaching. However, for education students, not only was the psychometrics course optional for their program, they did *not* need to take statistics as a prerequisite. The school set her up to fail, and there was little I could do about it.

In another institution where I taught assessment development at the graduate level to future and current teachers, the course was, again, *optional!* If you didn't have to take a course in a topic you didn't like or were afraid of, would you choose it? I sure wouldn't, especially if it also cost thousands of dollars. Thus, many of my students were coming to my class annoyed since the class was the only one that filled an elective requirement and fit in their schedule. For some of these students, undergraduate statistics was also optional, so they skipped the basics needed to understand the graduate-level content.

9   For those who opted out of this course, the Psychometric Society shares that "psychometrics is a scientific discipline concerned with the construction of assessment tools, measurement instruments, and formalized models that may serve to connect observable phenomena to theoretical attributes." This is fundamental for understanding educational assessment.

If this coursework is optional for educators, when are they supposed to learn the *assessment* part of curriculum, instruction, and assessment? With optional courses in critical topics of measurement and assessment, educational administrators and teachers are expected to use skills they never developed. It's like being hired to cook and you learned about all kinds of foods but you didn't learn how to use any of the kitchen tools or appliances. I suppose you could learn on the job and read the manuals.

So how many of your faculty can read and understand the technical manuals[10] that accompany assessments they use? How much money is spent on external testing programs that were not examined to make sure they measured what they were supposed to measure? Now, I don't expect all faculty to read them, but they should know the basics of psychometrics in order to understand the results they receive in instructional reports.

Understanding of basic measurement principles also impacts accurate grading, another task every teacher is required to perform. As Ken O'Connor discusses in *A Repair Kit for Grading: 15 Fixes for Broken Grades*, there are many practices that reduce the accuracy of grades from including non-academic indicators to giving a zero to missing work.[11] One calculation that generates inaccurate grades is the use of an arithmetic mean. If all of your faculty and student information systems are calculating averages using an arithmetic mean (i.e., the sum of the scores divided by the number of assessments), then I would ensure the instructional leaders review the topic of measures of central tendency *immediately*. A mean is accurate when the scores are normally distributed: not the class scores on the test, but rather the array of student scores over the course. Student scores are not always consistent with a normal distribution, so the better option is a median.[12]

10 A technical manual or report is developed for assessment tools to explain the psychometric underpinnings such as validity and reliability. The report should provide evidence that the tool does what it claims to do in the target population.

11 Giving a zero to a missed assignment means the student has zero knowledge or skill about the subject when in reality, you have no evidence to evaluate. If someone doesn't turn in an assignment in health class, does it really mean they know *nothing at all* about nutrition?

12 Extra nerd note: median equals mean in a normal distribution so a median is more accurate for every student.

In the following table, take a look at a student's performance over the course of the semester. Like many students, this student started low and improved as the semester progressed. For this student, a missing assignment was given a zero. Regardless of your philosophy about giving a zero, let's take a look at how using a more accurate calculation for a skewed dataset makes a difference. As you can see, the student did pretty well, except for that missing assignment. Using a mean to calculate the grade, the student gets a 76. Using a median, *the appropriate statistic for a skewed distribution*, the student gets an 85. The student gets almost *a whole grade* higher when the proper measurement is used!

We are doing a disservice to students when instructional staff lack basic measurement knowledge. Let me be more clear: *we are hurting students* when we don't use the right measurement approaches.

Student scores over the course of the semester: 76, 80, 0 (missing assignment), 85, 83, 87, 95, 88, 91	
Using Mean	*Using Median*
1) Sum of scores = 685	1) Reorder low to high: 0, 76, 80, 83, 85, 87, 88, 91, 95
2) Number of scores = 9	2) Find midpoint = 85
3) Calculate 685/9 = 76.1	3) Student earns a B
4) Student earns a C or C+	

Another example relates how the scores originate and how they can (or can't) be used. Some scores are based on percent correct and some are scale scores, like on the SAT, where a raw score is converted to a scale score. Usually this happens when item difficulty varies on an assessment. For years of my career, I've watched teachers take a scale score from a state test based on a 0-100 scale and combine it with their classroom test results based on percent correct. Since both go up to 100, what's the problem?

The problem is that the scales are not comparing apples to apples. Proficiency on the scale-scored test was 65 (which translates to about 30-40% correct due to varying item difficulty). Proficiency on a classroom test was 75%. Still not sure why we can't combine them? Let's change the scale score range from 55-100 to 900-100,000. Would teachers still be tempted to average the scores together?

I explained this problem by sharing the ideas of measuring temperature. If you take a bunch of temperatures using Fahrenheit and a bunch using Celsius, you'll get a set of numbers that measure temperature. However, since they are based on different scaling systems, if you combine them to determine average temperature, the result will not be accurate unless you convert one set of numbers. While many understood combining the temperatures before converting them to a common scale is a bad practice, they were reluctant (some even hostile) because averaging in the state test score into their classroom average was "something they always did." This issue combines lack of skills with lack of interest in changing (which we will dive into shortly).

When educators aren't trained in basic measurement principles, errors are made, and leaders like you are at risk for making decisions based on incorrect information. *Incorrect measurement practices lead to wrong decisions that hurt students.*

That's good data going bad.

Problem 3: People don't want to change.

I worked in a K12 education system where the English exit exams were offered in January and June. One school in particular gave the tests in June only and results were poor. Upon further investigation, it was discovered that the last few months before the June exam were spent taking practice tests—often, items pulled from old exams. There are a few problems with this practice.

The first problem with pulling items from old exams was that state exams were built using Item Response Theory (IRT) so some items were designed to be easy, while some were designed to be more difficult[13]. There is a good chance teachers were pulling items that were not along

---

13   There are a number of great online sites from research institutions that explain the item difficulty and item discrimination components of Item Response Theory in detail if you can't get enough of the topic.

the full range of difficulty. This error connects back to the previous section on the lack of learning about measurement in training programs.

The second problem was clear when I asked why the test wasn't given in January so the students who were proficient could be identified and those needing support mid-year could get academic intervention services. In response, a teacher asked "If the students all pass in January, what would we do the rest of the year?" Administering exams early could impact (i.e., require changing) what they taught so it was better in their eyes to keep doing what they were doing. Not very student-centered.

I've experienced additional mistakes made in institutions that prevented the access and use of the right data at the right time. Let's explore examples at every level—institutional, department or program, and classroom—as they'll have different implications for your work as a school leader.

At the Institutional Level

When I worked with a high school that had graduation rates between 70-80%, most of the students not graduating were dropping out[14]. It was clear that district leadership and external accountability systems wanted 100% of their students to persist to graduation. As the faculty and I discussed the work that might be needed to reduce dropout rates, one teacher said, "If we have a 100% graduation rate, where would we put all the students"? It turns out, the high school building was not designed to house all of their students in school until graduation!

So right away, there was little interest in reviewing data, making changes, and improving the learning environment because there was nowhere to put more students.[15]

---

14   In this state, graduation rate plus dropout rate did not always equal 100% due to other ways to complete the graduation requirements.

15   This is a great example of why facilities planning needs to be informed by the strategic plan.

At the Department/Program Level

A grant writer secures a nice chunk of funding for your student support services programming. In the proposal, it says that the program will improve student engagement, executive functioning, and social-emotional well-being as measured by the institution's social-emotional learning (SEL) assessment. The grant writer and the funding agency didn't know that your SEL tool doesn't measure engagement or executive functioning. When your team administers the assessment, the evaluators receive the data and tell you that you don't have enough information to provide feedback to the program staff or evidence to the funding agency. Now what?

Designing a program and evaluating its impact usually fall on two different people's to-do lists. When these people work like a relay team instead of like synchronized swimmers, there can be miscommunication. An example of this happened on an evaluation project I worked on. In the funded proposal created by a successful grant writing team, a reading test was listed to gauge writing skills when there was no writing portion on the reading test. At a department or program level, it's critical to develop measurement strategies 1) with the right people at the table and 2) when the objectives and activities are being developed. When this happens, you will have a well-choreographed result.

At the Classroom Level

I held a workshop with English faculty to review external test data, identify skills gaps, and review classroom assessments that contained the skills falling short so staff could be proactive in working on the areas where students struggled most. As the attendees were working on their crosswalk between the external test skills and their classroom assessment (a.k.a. item mapping), one veteran instructor asked for my assistance. She asked me to look at an item on her classroom test and tell her which learning standard it was measuring. I asked her which skill or standard she had in mind when she created the test. She told me that when she created the test, the learning standards were different. Some skills got moved to other grade levels so she wasn't responsible for them anymore while other skills had been added to her curriculum.

And there we have what I call the "Poltergeist Effect."

Do you remember the classic 1982 movie, *Poltergeist*? Spoiler alert coming: Toward the end of the movie, Steven, the dad character, confronts the land developer after supernatural entities take over his home, his child goes missing, and demonic violence is perpetrated against his family. He realizes these horrors are happening because the company built the housing development on a burial site without moving everything (or, should I say *everyone?*). He screams at the land developer:

> *"You moved the cemetery but you left the bodies…you left the bodies and you only moved the headstones! You only moved the headstones!"*

When I heard the teacher's comment about the curriculum changing, but the assessment not getting updated, I screamed in my head, "You changed the curriculum but you left the assessments! You only changed the curriculum! You only changed the curriculum!"

Clearly, the results from her classroom assessments would not help support students' skill development where it was needed most because not all of the skills were being measured. Thus, even if she was using classroom data to drive instruction, she could be looking at the wrong skills.

Reflection

We've reviewed the reasons that schools don't utilize good information that is available. Time may be limited, skills may be lacking, and there may be little interest in changing the way things have always been done. These limitations add error to decision-making, and in Part II you'll learn how to keep good data from going bad through activities that maximize time, re-energize staff, and focus attention on what is best for students.

Which obstacles do you recognize that are getting in the way of using data effectively in your school?

How many of these are present at your institution?

- ☐ Limited time for data collection and analysis
- ☐ Faculty and administration without education or training in measurement
- ☐ Reluctance to change classroom practices based on evidence
- ☐ Plans implemented without evaluation practices identified
- ☐ Changes in curriculum without updating assessments

Okay, at this point you know how easy isn't always effective and how different limitations at your school can ruin good data. In the next chapter, we'll take a look at how schools struggle to bring people along due to deep-seated attitudinal issues. Positive school improvement efforts can be quickly derailed by negative attitudes about using evidence. Grab a pen and paper (we still love school supplies), and let's identify how negative attitudes can be a source of error that impedes success in your school.

CHAPTER 3

The Other Four-Letter Word

LET'S PLAY A WORD ASSOCIATION GAME. GRAB A sheet of paper. I'm going to give you three words related to schools, and I want you to write down the *first* word that enters your mind when you see them.

You may have somewhat mixed feelings about any one of these terms, but write down your *first* thought or reaction. Ready?

Word number one is: *library*. How does that word make you feel? What comes to mind when you see this word? Did the word you wrote down have a positive or negative sentiment?

Your next word is: *accountability*. How does that word make you feel? What comes to mind when you see this word? Did the word you wrote down have a positive or negative sentiment?

Your final word is: *data*. How does that word make you feel? What comes to mind when you see this word? Did the word you wrote down have a positive or negative sentiment?[16]

Let's focus on the last word prompt, *data*. I call it "the other four-letter word" because the word *data* also causes people to raise eyebrows, shake their heads, and even mutter under their breath in disgust.

What were *your* initial reactions to the word, *data*? Some people love it, others not so much. It is kind of like broccoli. At first sight, some people will make a face and say "no thanks" before you ask if they want it. Others are excited to see their favorite veggie.

How can you get those who dislike it to tolerate it? They might not become broccoli champions, but you don't want them to have a gag

---

16   Send your list of three words to me at hello@allabreveconsulting.com. I'll post a sentiment analysis to our email newsletter after I receive enough responses.

reflex at the site of a green floret. How would you get others to eat broccoli if they say they don't like it? Would you hide it in a casserole? Would you discuss all of the health benefits of broccoli? Would you negotiate a trade or reward them if they eat it?

In education, you can't hide data. They are everywhere! You might already talk about how important they are and reward staff with time or stipends to get them to review data. Yet, you do these things and people are still negative, and it impacts their ability to be successful with students.

I know from my experience in K12 and higher education that the word "data" doesn't always generate a warm fuzzy feeling in the hearts of educators. Think about it: when was the last time you told your team you were going to meet to review data, and the collective response was "YAY!" – and not in a sarcastic way. When your teachers are asked to provide evidence of learning that will provide insight about skills development and not just a grade on an assignment, do they respond with enthusiasm or indifference? In my many years of working with teachers and administrators in the use of data to drive decisions, it is the rare occasion that the institutional culture looks at data as fun and not frustrating.

Why does this matter? As the saying goes, misery loves company. In reality, the research shows that misery loves *miserable* company (Schachter, 1959). People use the cues of others to reinforce their own feelings, so those who are negative may seek to build support for their outlook. And we know that one bad apple can spoil the bunch. In this chapter, we'll uncover the signs of those apples in your school so you can work on saving the bunch.

The Origins of Negativity

The longer a negative attitude is in place, the harder it will be to change (Johnson et al, 2022). In my years of teaching statistics and training teachers on using data, I've heard some really bad attitudes about the subject matter. Some negative attitudes were generated during childhood experiences and carried into adulthood (and the education profession), so they will be more difficult to change. Others were formed while working in education, often influenced by those bad apples we mentioned earlier.

When attitudes are negative and long-standing, they impact behavior. If you have a negative attitude about exercise, it's going to be a challenge to hit your wellness goal if you need to exercise! In education, negative attitudes about using evidence to improve student success will impact your staff's ability to implement the right strategies to improve student success because *they need to use data to design and evaluate those efforts.*

Knowing where the negative attitudes originate will help you navigate your team toward positive outcomes. If the attitude was formed prior to employment in your school, the culture you establish will be critical to foster positive behaviors. If the attitude was formed or reinforced while working in your school, you will have another set of opportunities ahead. In Part II, you'll learn how to build that culture; for now, you need to be aware of the barriers you may encounter.

You are never going to have a school full of data cheerleaders, but knowing where the negativity comes from and how it impacts others working to support students will help you minimize the chance of making the wrong decisions for your students. In the following sections, we'll see how negative attitudes about data emerge and the impact can have on your institution's success.

Negative Experiences in Classes About Statistics

To this day, I hear from people who shudder at the memory of their statistics courses, telling me, "I hated that class." With additional discussion, they recollect the formulas or the fast pace or say they were always bad at math. For many, the class also ended with a grade lower than what they earned in their other, more "enjoyable" classes.

Then, I typically tell them that they just didn't have the right teacher. Why did I jump to that conclusion? For a subject that is challenging, confusing, or scary, it is up to the instructor to make the material relevant, providing a *context* for the content. Giving the challenging content context and relevance provides *meaning* for students. Without relevance, students become disengaged, will forget what they learned, and may have reduced motivation.[17] How many of your staff perceived the content in their statistics courses as irrelevant or disconnected from their career, assuming they were even required to take those classes?

In school when students aren't engaged in the content, they will do whatever it takes to just get it over with (assuming they don't skip or drop the course). When staff members sit in your data meetings with negative attitudes forged from disengaged classroom experiences of their own, they will do what it takes to "just be done" with the data conversation or task. They will forget what was discussed in the meeting and go back to the classroom to keep doing what they were already doing.

Negative Experiences in the Workplace

When disengaged, staff won't want to use data to improve outcomes. And when data are used for punitive purposes instead of for improvement insights, it can make staff frustrated, fearful, or annoyed in the short term and may reduce morale and motivation to make evidenced-based decisions in the long term.

Punitive performance evaluation systems are not new. At a state level, schools may lose funding if they don't make progress when they really need to receive additional funding to close performance gaps. This funding punishment is likely to result in decreased motivation or attempts to discredit the evaluation system when schools have to do more with less.

At a classroom level, punitive use of course evaluations can also impact motivation. The purpose of end of course evaluations should be to provide feedback to the instructor regarding what was useful as well as what was unclear, difficult, or frustrating. This information could and

17   Sara Bernard, "Science Shows Making Lessons Relevant Really Matters." Edutopia, December 1, 2010, https://www.edutopia.org/neuroscience-brain-based-learning-relevance-improves-engagement.

should lead to changes in future courses that will make learning more impactful and students more successful. But what if the course evaluation results determined salary increases or tenure decisions? In a Reddit thread that asked what would change if evaluations weren't tied to consequences, some responses indicated that evaluations did not matter to their teaching while others indicated they would give more feedback to students, grade harder, or be more experimental in approaches to the curriculum. One comment even discredited the evaluations, stating "students are not qualified to rate pedagogy." Another comment said removing course evaluations would lead to feeling "supported by [the] institution" and "increase motivation level."

With pressure in the workplace due to accountability systems designed to punish instead of support, it's clear to see how the use of data "for evil" will interfere with wanting to use data "for good."

Lack of Exposure or Practice Using Data Productively

Earlier we discussed that many educators are not being exposed to measurement principles during their graduate education. When staff begin careers at their institutions, they might not get sufficient exposure to or practice in the proper use of data to drive decisions. From assessment design to grade calculations to evaluating program effectiveness, there is no shortage of evidenced-based decisions. Without someone watching their measurement backs, there are too many opportunities for staff to be misinformed or duped into doing things that hurt student success. And if your team feels misled by data, their attitudes toward evidence-based decisions will sour.

It is common for a school to form a data team as a reaction to a book study or external accountability requirement. I've seen staff with great knowledge of their content areas and pedagogy get reassigned to be in charge of these data activities. Why? Sometimes because no one else wanted to do it or because the institution wanted to keep the person employed after instructional cuts. Being assigned to the data role won't get the person caught up on principles of measurement and psychometrics unless it is part of the requirements of the position. And it rarely is.

As an administrator supporting K12 schools, I witnessed vendors try to take advantage of school staff's measurement shortcomings. In one presentation to building leaders, the vendor said the assessment tool they were selling would predict the results on the new state tests: a claim that got the group's attention! This was an interesting statement since the state tests were still in development and were not scheduled to be administered for another year. So for measurement-naïve ears, the claim sounded great, *but without past data from similar state tests, how did they build the predictive model?* That was the question I asked because I had their measurement backs.

The vendor response? Well, the rep said they were working on it. Further, he hoped schools would agree to share their results from the new tests with the company in order to do the work to build the models. With a mental facepalm, I placed my pen on the table, folded my arms, and sat back in my chair. They had *nothing*—no evidence to support their claims—yet they made the claim because they expected the audience to be without the knowledge to question them! If the schools at the table purchased the assessment software and tried to use the results to guide instruction based on the predicted test scores, they could end up wasting time and money on strategies that weren't appropriate for the students.

As another example, administrators at a K12 school district wanted to implement a new reading program, and fortunately the program had a technical report to share about the effectiveness of the program. It was full of tables and statistical jargon, so I asked if I could review it (I really do love reviewing technical reports). In the section where it talked about whether or not students in the program did better than students not in the program, the finding was that: *students in the program performed better but the difference was not statistically significant.* And the words "performed better" were what they emphasized with **bold** letters. Wow. So what that meant was: the results of students in the program were higher than the results of students not in the program, *but not high* *enough to be due to the impact of the program versus due to chance.* In other words, the program did not make a difference. I told the district to carefully consider their purchase since the claims of improved performance as a result of the program were not supported by the evidence *the company provided.*

In these examples, educators were at risk for making the wrong decisions about student performance that could have detrimental effects on engagement and success. How can your team use data productively and make the right choices for students if no one has the school's measurement best interests in mind and are not in the room when these dysfunctional discussions are happening?

Others' Negative Perceptions of Data, Statistics, or Math in General

"My [insert family member] always struggled with math." "My friends told me statistics is the hardest course." Hearing co-workers complain about "having to review data." The more negative your social groups are about the idea of "doing data," the more it can impact your attitudes about it and ultimately shape behaviors.

Did you know that even strangers with negative attitudes can influence someone's decisions? In the classic study on social conformity, people gave wrong information to go along with the crowd, even when they knew the right answer.

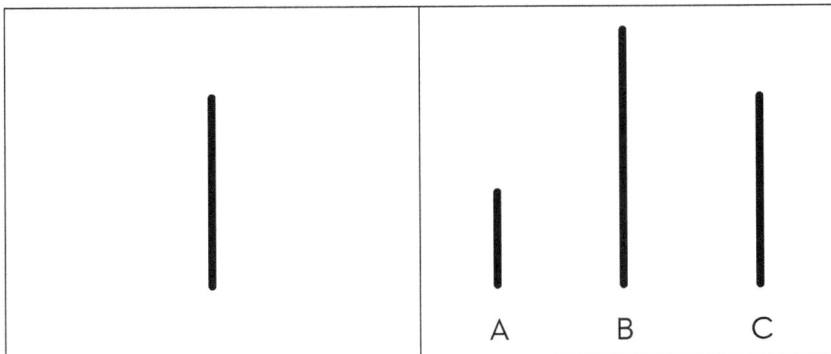

Figure 1: Line Test from Asch Study (1951)

In the figure above from the research study, you can see clearly that the line on the left matches line C on the right; however, when the group majority stated a different line as the match, subjects tended to agree with the group instead of going with the right answer! In schools, staff (particularly untenured) may go along with the group who has the loudest voice, even if that voice is wrong.

When others, like family members, tenured faculty colleagues, or even a group of strangers think negatively about data, statistics, or math in general, your staff can be influenced to go against the right insights. In education, when a new staff member arrives at the school or perhaps someone attends a conference and is faced with negative attitudes and opinions about using data, it's not unusual for the negative attitudes to influence the new person who might not want to stand out as different from others. The social pressure to conform will have a harmful effect on student outcomes.

In each of these four origins of negativity, the impact on your student success is at stake. Now, you might not know the data origin story of each of your staff members, but you will see the manifestations of these experiences. In the next section, we'll review what to look for in your school. If you're seeing these types of behaviors from your staff, consider if the origins of their negativity are long-standing or created within your hallways and conference rooms. The more potentially harmful attitudes you can identify, the quicker you can make adjustments so students are not caught in a web spun from negativity.

Types of Data-Averse Educators

Because of negative attitudes about data (however they are formed), I've witnessed data-averse educators 1) avoid discussions or activities that require using data, 2) go through the motions, particularly when the work is for external accountability or accreditation, or 3) even argue against using data. When these behaviors happen, it's a clear sign of bad decisions ahead. Those bad decisions impact students' experiences at the institution, and ultimately keep your school from achieving its potential. To help you identify when success is going to be stymied, let's explore each of these types of data-averse educators.

Which do you recognize in *your* institution?

Data Evaders

As stated by Keith Cunningham in *The Road Less Stupid*,

> "We live in a world where accountability and measuring are feared and avoided."

Data Evaders in education manage to avoid discussions or deflect conversations regarding measurement or analysis. They may be intentionally absent from the meeting or send someone else in their place. When it's time to select sessions to attend at a professional development day or conference, they rarely choose data or research-based topics.

A Data Evader's behavior sometimes mimics liars who are trying to convince you about something. A Harvard Business School article (Nobel, 2013) stated, "liars tended to use many more words…than did truth tellers, presumably in an attempt to win over suspicious receivers." So you may notice Data Evaders try to convince you they love data by giving you too many details about unrelated (even if important) work. When attending a meeting to present evidence about a program, they may double down on the instructional minutiae or fill the conversation with anecdotal evidence about how much students love coming to the program.

For example, I witnessed a school leader who was supposed to be providing a *brief* update about quarterly achievements. Instead, the administrator shared every tiny detail about the program implementation and proposed timeline of activities for the rest of the year. This report lasted over an hour. It was all fluff, no stuff; a clear Data Evader who needs to know what evidence is truly important.

Passive Participants

You've been in professional development sessions where attendees are mentally checked out. In fact, you may have been *that* attendee at one point. I admit, I've been there myself. In the case of the Passive Participant, the person is sitting at the table, but their engagement level is low, they just want to get the task done, or they are the "yes" people who agree with whatever someone else is doing. Do you find any team members acquiescing to the loudest voice in the room or the HIPPO (highest paid person's opinion) when evidence is the topic of conversation?

Often, I see this type of behavior when staff members are told they have to attend a session or when there is work needed for an external group (e.g., state report, accreditation, or external evaluator). They do not see the impact of participating in these sessions on their work except as a disruption to their day. I have fond memories (sarcasm alert) of leading an in-service day when the staff were supposed to be reviewing their students' information and designing lessons to address gaps. At least two teachers were on Facebook on the school computers. Their behavior didn't hurt my feelings; instead my heart hurt for their students who were not getting the education they deserved. A Passive Participant is checked out and needs a new way to check back in.

Data Antagonists

In my first major role at an institution where I was tasked with collecting all sorts of data for program evaluation, accountability, and accreditation, I was literally backed against a wall after a faculty meeting by one of the instructional staff. In short, the instructor asked what I thought I was doing and let me know that my work and my data were not welcome there. *That* was a fun day.

As a social psychologist, I was curious what attitudes and social norms may have led to that unnecessarily aggressive behavior. What was at the core of the Data Antagonist mindset? What might lead to someone on your staff to be oppositional or confrontational in the presence of a data discussion?

Thinking of the classic frustration-aggression hypothesis (Dollard et al, 1939), if someone is blocked from attaining a goal, there can be frustration, followed by aggression. The aggression is a proxy for the true reason the person is frustrated. Once the aggression act releases emotions, the person feels relief, a catharsis. For the aggressive instructor, the goal was to keep the status quo. Reviewing data (with my office facilitating) was seen as a threat to the status quo. Thus, if this person had keeping the status quo as a goal, my office would continue to be a target of angry outbursts. The Data Antagonist needs a new goal or a different focus.

Reflection

Even if you identify what your students need to achieve success and get through the challenges presented in the last chapter, you may hit obstacles due to negative attitudes toward data. These negative attitudes add error to the decision-making process and have a detrimental effect on success.

Throughout this chapter, we revealed the source of negative attitudes toward all things data and identified how those feelings often manifest in your school. We talked about how long-standing negative attitudes are harder to change and are strengthened when surrounded by similarly negative people. As these attitudes turn into problem behaviors in your school, it's critical that you address them early and often. The more they persist, the more they will impair decisions that will affect students.

In recent years, I've (thankfully) experienced less overt aggression from **Data Antagonists**. However, frustration around evidence-based decision-making persists due to negative experiences, lack of exposure or practice, or the influence of others. Avoidance like a **Data Evader** or passive-aggressive behaviors like complaining on social media from a **Passive Participant** are more common ways educators express frustration with evidence-based practices. The root of the frustration is what needs to be addressed—the goal or focus of your team—and we will explore that in Part II of the book.

Which of the following "data-averse educator" types do you have at your institution? What percentage of the overall school community do they comprise?

- ☐ Data Evaders _____%
- ☐ Passive Participants _____%
- ☐ Data Antagonists _____%

PART II

Changing the Data Culture

In Part I of this book, you learned about the kinds of errors that can occur when schools don't do the right things regarding evidence. If your school uses easy instead of effective approaches to collecting and analyzing data, you will have error in your decisions. If your school has limited time, skill, or interest regarding sound measurement practices, you will have error in your decisions. If you have staff with negative perceptions about data, there will be obstacles in your journey to evidence-based decisions. Each of these challenges leads to wrong insights that lead to wrong decisions that hurt students. And that's why people think your school sucks. In Part II, you'll learn what you and your school can do to fix it.

Instead of the ABCs that you are used to hearing about in schools, Part II presents the *DEFs* of changing your institution's culture around evidence-based decisions. D stands for **Discussion**, and you'll learn how to get everyone clear about *what* success means for your institution. If there is clear communication and consensus about the definition of success (or any desired outcome), then everyone can work toward the same end result. E is for **Exploration**, and you'll see the importance of getting your team to identify *which* results matter most. If there is effort to review the right data in the right atmosphere, everyone is aware if progress is being made. Identifying key performance indicators ensures progress is being tracked and the school held accountable for the right results. F is for **Focus**: without a clear vision about *how* your school will achieve success, there is little chance your school will get there. If there is a single priority area that all efforts are focused toward, then everyone is contributing to the same goal and decisions are made based on what is most important. When there are too many competing tasks, the school won't maximize its resources for the greatest gains.

Think about our wellness[18] example again. You and your family (or trainer or therapist) *discuss* what wellness means for you with a clear definition of what successful wellness looks like: more energy, better sleep, and the need for fewer prescriptions. Next you *explore* the key metrics you will track like sleep patterns, protein and carbohydrate intake, blood pressure, and water consumption. Then your wellness plan for the next year has a singular *focus*, like reversing heart disease, so your actions are targeted. By incorporating strategies to reverse heart disease, you will impact your wellness outcomes, tracked by your key metrics.

By using the DEF approach in schools, you will get to higher levels of success without getting stuck. Remember that just like in wellness work, if it were easy to do, *everybody would be doing it already*. It will take some work, necessary work, to implement all three. This is critical: without all three—*discussion, exploration, and focus*—your school won't measure up. Let's look at each scenario where one is missing to see what I mean.

D-E Without F

This is where I see many schools veer off course. They talk a lot about the data, but do not have a shared priority, so it's easy to just continue doing the same things or get overwhelmed by the chaos of competing priorities. The staff does what it has always done, and trust is eroded over time. Little purposeful progress is made.

E-F Without D

In this example, school teams are reviewing data incorrectly or inconsistently since they haven't defined what the desired outcomes are. They can't see what success should look like so they set a plan that doesn't connect to the ultimate desired results. People can see that everyone is working hard and might be confused why desired outcomes are still

---

18   Please note I am not a medical professional and this paragraph is for illustration only; it should not be viewed as medical advice.

falling short. The school is siloed, and frustration builds over time as efforts don't produce results.

D–F Without E

In this combination, there is a lot of planning work and goal setting, but the measurement of progress is missing or disconnected from the desired outcomes. The school has a plan, they just don't track the plan. As years pass, they wonder why their efforts "didn't work." This school thinks it is proactive, but ends up being reactive because they explored results too late—if at all. This leads to frustration with the planning process, teams demotivated from continuing down the path toward success, and a negative view of leadership.

Do any of these descriptions sound like your school? In any of these scenarios, we experience some of the DEF elements. In a functional data culture, the entire DEF process exists and persists. The important takeaway is that if your institution cuts out ONE of the pieces, then it is missing something that's critical to achieving success and realizing its mission.

Without discussion, exploration, and *focus, your school won't measure up.* Goals won't be attained; success will remain out of reach. And people will continue to think your school sucks.

Let's make sure that doesn't happen.

CHAPTER 4

Changing the Culture—
Discussion

THINK OF YOUR LEADERSHIP TEAM AS MEMBERS OF an elite rowing crew. It's critical that each member of the team rows with purpose, aiming for a specific direction. What happens if one person decides to row a different way?

If just one person rows a different way, there's a good chance the team will still get where they want to go, but it could take a lot longer to get there. If too many members of the team are going in different directions, the boat could spin around and never get to where it wants to go.

In the same way, if your institution doesn't agree on a clear idea of what result everyone should be aiming for, it can't reach its goals for success. School teams are usually pretty good at setting goals, but my experience has shown that these goals often operate like a rowing team going in different directions. There's a lot going on but not a lot getting done.

To stop your team from spinning in circles, you need to get crystal clear about what is expected from the institution's goals. To make the most progress toward these goals, everyone at your institution or school community needs to agree on what success looks like for the students it serves. We'll call this "success criteria."

To achieve consensus on the success criteria, stakeholders need to stop, collaborate, and listen.[19] This is where the DEFs of changing culture around evidence-based decisions starts: with *Discussion*. The school community—staff, students, families, and others—need to be on the same page about what success means for students; that is, what does it look like. They need to know what the success criteria are so that they can determine whether or not their efforts accomplished the desired outcomes. Discussions that make success criteria clear will keep your team from spinning out of control.

ATTENTION PLEASE

If your school has any of the following based on your reflections checklist from Part I, this chapter will be important for your work.

- ☐ Outdated and/or extremely general mission statement
- ☐ Focus on outputs over outcomes
- ☐ Lack of agreement about what success indicators are
- ☐ Reluctance to change classroom practices based on evidence
- ☐ Plans implemented without evaluation practices identified
- ☐ Changes in curriculum without updating assessments
- ☐ Passive Participants

Getting Clear

In schools that don't have a clear definition of success, there is little agreement of what success looks like, so they default to collecting evidence based on what's easy to get instead of what's effective at addressing success criteria. Then, at the end of the year, they don't know why they haven't met their goals. "But we taught that," "But we had a good turnout," "But we spent a lot of time training on…" and the list goes on. These are outputs, not outcomes. They don't achieve results because they don't know what outcomes matter because they haven't defined what success should look like first.

19   Yes, that's a Vanilla Ice reference.

Most education professionals have heard the Stephen Covey habit, "begin with the end in mind." In Covey's work, one needs to create a mental image and then set the course of action to make it happen. In schools, if a goal is to ensure students are prepared for careers, and your faculty teaches a new career exploration curriculum, then what? Then we need to know if the program was successful; that is, what students now know and can do as a result of the program. If it isn't clear what the end result should look like, the teachers don't know if the curriculum is actually preparing students for future careers. If there is no evidence the new career curriculum leads to more preparation because the impact wasn't measured, it's easy to say, "Well, that didn't work" or "We should just do things the way we always did."

I've seen this disconnect when I hear higher education faculty talk about how incoming first year students are not ready for college-level content. This lack of readiness often leads to students being required to take developmental (or pre-college) courses that cost money but don't generate credits toward graduation. Meanwhile, at the secondary level, teachers and administrators point to the students passing exit exams and declare they are prepared. With this view of the evidence, secondary staff have little motivation to change what they have always done. In speaking to audiences in K12 and higher education, I've emphasized that the minimum to graduate high school does not necessarily equate to the minimum to enter college. Can the two sides come to consensus about what "college ready" really means so students can be more successful?

When schools are clear on what success looks like, everyone is rowing in the same direction. Is your team having effective discussions that define success criteria so all rowers are in sync? Imagine your team decides that *trust* is an issue to be addressed in your strategic plan. What does trust mean to your staff? Is everyone defining it the same way? How do you know when trust is better? In one school I worked with, trust was on the strategic planning table. They met as a leadership team, with administration and faculty, to identify elements of trust. I noticed one person (we will call him Max) who wasn't involved in the discussion, so at the break I checked in. "How is it going, Max? I see you've been quiet. Is there something I can do differently after the break?" Max said it wasn't me or the activity per se, but the fact that Max was fearful if he said something others didn't like, they would hold it against him after the session. Trust issues ran so deep they couldn't even discuss how to define it!

After this feedback, I reworked the activity to ensure each person could provide input[20] into the definition of trust that would define success criteria. In this school, one part of the trust definition had to be making sure staff members at every level feel they could speak freely without fear of retribution. At the end of the day, I checked back in with Max. He smiled with relief and felt the definition would resonate with those who weren't present and felt the same as he did. With a clear definition and activities that were tied to agreed-upon elements of trust, he felt the school had a better chance of success. A while after this session, I checked in on the institution's progress. Because they had clear definitions of trust that were used to establish success criteria, they were able to link efforts to results. Trust in that school isn't perfect, but it is making solid progress in the right direction.

Discussion + Definition = Direction

On the surface, you and I both have an idea of what trust looks like. But as an institution, how do you know you built a culture of trust? There is a famous line from the 1993 movie *And the Band Played On* that chronicled the origins of the AIDS epidemic. Before jumping to a conclusion, one doctor would ask others, "What do we think, what do we know, what can we prove?" This question set addressed the challenge of having an idea versus being able to measure it. Creating discussions that clarify definitions of success help with the "think" and "know" questions, but what about the "prove" question? In the last chapter, we talked about how what we think and know connect to outputs and

---

20 A good way to do this is to have individuals write their ideas on a sticky note and then organize the sticky notes by theme. Everyone has input and no one knows who contributed which idea.

outcomes. Now we need to consider "prove," that is, how we collect evidence about what we think we know.

Getting clear about what needs to be measured helps you get the proof you need to confirm your efforts are headed in the right direction. There have been many strategic planning sessions when I worked with school leaders, and they stopped short of articulating the goals and objectives that matter most to their institution because, in their words, "you can't measure *that*." My response is always, "You can measure anything!"[21] *We have to be very clear about what we want to accomplish so that we can measure it.* This requires a shared definition or, even better, *an operational definition*, of the construct.

What is a Construct?

The term *construct* represents multiple ideas that combine to create it. You can't see the construct without looking at the things that it represents.

Let's use the construct of "furniture." You can't see it without thinking of pieces of furniture. What came to your mind? A chair, bed, desk, table, ottoman? You can envision these items, and when combined, they fall under the construct of furniture.

There could even be sub-constructs like living room furniture, dining room furniture, and bedroom furniture. Some items, like a chair, might appear in multiple sub-constructs. If you clarify that the chair is a recliner, then it is more likely to be added to the living room furniture group.

The more specific you are, the more clear your construct becomes. And the more specific it is, the more your team can share your idea of what furniture means and execute that idea.

An operational definition (Stephens, 1935) describes the construct using descriptions based on how it can be observed and even measured. For example, the operational definition of anxiety could be a score on a test, avoiding an activity, elevated heart rate, perspiration, or even a

---

21   And this became the name of my podcast; we will revisit it in the conclusion.

combination of these. For any construct (like trust), educational leaders have to be clear about what it looks like *and what it doesn't look like* to ensure that the measurement tools align to those descriptors. *If we can't "see" it, we can't measure it.*

Some constructs are easier to define, and some are more difficult, but all can be clarified and calculated if you follow the five steps outlined in this section. Once your team has discussed what success (or any hard-to-measure construct) means for your institution, your organization will be able to understand what matters most and implement strategies that stop the boat from spinning and move everyone closer to the finish line.

Remember: you can't measure it accurately if you can't define it.

Drawing from my background in social science research and decades of working in schools, I came up with this five-step process for measuring anything so you can take any construct (e.g., effective communication, resilience, or trust) and figure out how to measure it.

The five steps are:

1. *What is the construct you want to measure?*
2. *How do others define and/or measure it?*
3. *What does it look like in your school?*
4. *What doesn't it look like in your school?*
5. *Summarize.*

Let's walk through each step with an example that pops up in just about every school in some way. Using this example, you will learn the questions that will help facilitate discussions so you can be clear on your success criteria[22]. Once there is consensus about the definition of the construct, you will be in a better place to create plans that get you to the desired outcomes, with everyone rowing in the same direction.

---

22   For a video example of this process, visit *www.yourschoolsucks.com/resources*.

1. What is the construct you want to measure?

Satisfaction? Engagement? Happiness? Love? Any one of these concepts is measurable. First, what is the construct commonly called at your institution? What do employees call it? What do students call it? What about parents/families, alumni, and the community?

Let's use *engagement*, specifically family engagement. Maybe your leadership team calls it engagement, parents call it *involvement*, and staff think of it as *participation*. Are there other ways your team or your stakeholders refer to that concept? Would new staff members or students call it something different? List the ways that people inside and outside of the institution refer to the idea of being engaged with the school.

Next, is it a *head concept* or a *heart concept*? That is, does the idea reflect someone's thoughts, feelings, or a combination? Love might be considered more "heart" based since it is associated with emotional reactions, and interest might be considered more "head" based since it requires paying attention and thinking about something. Engagement could be considered a bit of both since, to be fully engaged, one has to be aware (head concept) of the opportunity and want (heart concept) to be involved. This distinction will play a role in steps three and four.

Go ahead and make a list of all of the ways people refer to family engagement in your school community. We aren't looking for a definition until the next step; now we are capturing how people talk about the concept. When you do this in a group discussion, it's helpful to get a wide variety of perspectives related to the construct. You can also get more thoughts by using variations of the word, like "engaged" or "engaging."[23]

2. How do others define and/or measure it?

If I do a search for the term "engagement," I'll find a *lot* of definitions and synonyms, and perhaps I might even discover some existing tools for measuring engagement. First, find a definition from existing research

---

23   If you are so inclined, you can also run your term through an AI tool to get other ways people talk about your construct.

that most resembles what the term means to your organization. Perhaps you find a definition of employee engagement that states it is:

The level of enthusiasm and dedication a worker feels toward their job.[24]

Furthermore,

Engaged employees care about their work and about the performance of the company, and feel that their efforts make a difference.

From this source, you might need to consider enthusiasm, dedication, care, and feeling useful as part of the definition of family engagement.

Next, collect a few examples of surveys, checklists, or articles that relate to the construct, if available. There are many surveys and checklists about engagement that might inform your definition and direction. How many of them connect to the desired characteristics of enthusiasm, dedication, care, and feeling useful?

Finally, does the research link the construct to other ideas? That is, what might be related to the construct of interest and what might it have an impact on? For example, engagement might impact satisfaction or attendance. Are these the outcomes that the institution wants to impact and the *real* reason engagement was chosen as important? Tracking potential outcomes of satisfaction and attendance will help clarify how your organization will measure it.

This step will take a little more time than the last one. Employee engagement may look different than student engagement or family engagement, just like living room furniture may look different from bedroom furniture. Teasing out the differences will help you communicate these ideas more clearly and will ensure they are measured appropriately. Spend time with representatives of your school community to find out

24 Tim Smith, "What Is Employee Engagement? Definition, Strategies, and Example," Investopedia, June 20, 2024. *www.investopedia.com/terms/e/employee-engagement.asp.*

how these sub-constructs match or differ. Without clarity here, your boat will start to turn.

3. *What does it look like in your organization?*

In this step, we want to break down the construct into observables that anyone can agree upon. This is where you get operational definition-y. We need to consider what is observed when there is an "engaged" parent (could be another family member but we will use the term parent for this set of questions) on the school campus or in other activities related to school. Envision the parent who would win the title of "most engaged." Start by asking:

> a) How do you know the parent is engaged when you see the person? Would your colleagues agree?

List everything you see the parent *doing* that shows engagement. Some observables might be: wearing school logo items, attending open house events, or volunteering for school committees. If someone uses the phrase, "active listening," you need to probe more. How do you know they are actively listening if you are only observing? Could you look like you are actively listening if you aren't paying attention?

> b) Is the behavior a reflection of a thought or idea ("head" based) or is it a reflection of a feeling or motivation ("heart" based)? Which drove the behavior more?

For engagement, is the behavior an expression of a belief about the organization or about a feeling/emotion? Many of the observed behaviors listed in the section above are manifestations of emotions more than thoughts. Being knowledgeable about opportunities to get involved is more head-based, and wearing logo merch to show school pride is more heart-based.

c) Is it a number of something? That is, was the behavior observed a certain number of times?

Earlier we said that engagement might be related to attendance so perhaps the number of times the person is present or absent might be an indicator of engagement. Another behavior could be the number of times the parent asks a related question.

d) Amount of something? Is engagement based on how much of a characteristic you see?

When the construct can be measured by the amount of something present, we can identify levels of engagement. For example, the amount of time a parent talks to staff or peers about school improvement could be a way to determine if the parent is slightly engaged or very engaged.

e) Something present or not?

This one is more binary—the behavior is present or not. For engagement, a behavior like eye contact with the administrator might mean engaged and lack of eye contact might mean not engaged.

Keep in mind that one behavior alone does not define the construct.

4. What doesn't it look like in your school?

Following up on the last part of part three, what does it look like when the concept is *absent* in your school? In our example, if someone is *not* engaged, what actions or behaviors do you observe? Are they a function of beliefs (head-based) or emotions (heart-based)?

There's a popular student engagement scene in the movie *Ferris Bueller's Day Off* when the teacher is giving a lesson, and it's evident there is a lack of engagement in the classroom from the behaviors of the students. If you aren't familiar with the scene, one student stares blankly with mouth agape, another is staring while holding a pen in their open mouth, and a third is also looking at the teacher with wide eyes, not blinking and mouth hanging open. Additional students are shown with similar blank expressions: one has her chin on her hands on her desk with tired eyes blinking slowly and one is completely asleep with a trail of saliva streaming across the desktop. Even if we didn't hear or see the instructor, we can tell there is a lack of engagement in the classroom by the collection of observable behaviors.

What are the telltale signs that a parent isn't engaged? Is the parent absent from conferences and events? Does the parent ask questions about school happenings on social media when the information was already shared through parent portals? Does the parent spread rumors about the school on social media?

5. Summarize.

Based on your responses to the above steps, you should be able to summarize your construct in observable terms.

The format of our summary is:

We know that _____ is present in our school/ with our stakeholders (students, staff, etc.) because we see them _____, and they no longer are _____.

For family engagement in a school, we might say:

We know that engagement is present with our parents because we see them spending more time in our building, asking staff questions, and sharing accurate information about the institution on social media, and they no longer skip parent conferences or sending negative emails to the administration.

We might even think of the impact of parent engagement on student behaviors such as attendance, disruptions, being prepared for class, etc. If parent engagement exists as evidenced by the characteristics above, then student behavior may change in ways that can be measured as well.

Reflection

With these steps, you now have an approach to measure any concept that matters to your institution. If there is clear communication and consensus about what success means, then everyone is moving toward the same result. *Remember, discussion plus definition equals direction.*

Now it's *your* turn. In the following pages, you'll find these questions to guide your discussion. There is a downloadable worksheet at www.yourschoolsucks.com/resources. Use this process to define what success and any other important construct means to your school community, and then proceed to the next chapter.

1. What is the construct you want to measure?

☐ *What do the employees of the institution call it?*
☐ *What do others call it?*
☐ *Is it related to the head (thoughts) or the heart (feelings)?*

2. How do others define and/or measure it?

3. What does it look like in your school?

☐ *How do you know it when you see it?*
☐ *What would you "show" to others?*

4. What doesn't it look like in your school?

☐ *How do you know it is not present?*
☐ *What are people doing that show you it's not there?*

5. Summarize.

We know that _____ is present in our school/ with our stakeholders (students, staff, etc.) because we see them _____, and they no longer are _____.

CHAPTER 5

Changing the Culture—
Exploration

"Action is the foundational key to all success."
PABLO PICASSO

IMAGINE YOU ARE RUNNING A WEIGHT LOSS PROGRAM
and you have people exercising and cutting calories. Is that success? Before you choose the right workouts and the right nutritional balance, you need data to know where participants start and determine where you want them to be at the end of the program. Then, as you implement actions, you check progress.

If only a handful of people in the program have this insight or maybe just you as the program coordinator knows the participant data, will participants get to their desired results? If I didn't know what I needed to track to reach my goal and felt the need to record water intake, step counts, every vitamin and nutrient, every calorie consumed, every calorie burned, grams of carbs consumed, grams of protein, etc., it would get exhausting. I'd probably give up, or maybe even avoid the program or the people in it.

Which data points are *most* important to achieving my goal? It depends on where I start and where I want to be. I need to be aware of the key data points as well as be comfortable tracking them to show progress toward my goal.

While Picasso said action is the key to success, I think it is critical to have the *right* key to unlock the *right* door to achieve success. The way to make sure your actions are the right ones for your school is with the data. I don't mean just *any* data. Choosing any available data is what leads to problems like using easy over effective approaches to analysis, being reactive to accountability requirements instead of being proactive, or avoiding the data completely because it is just too much work.

With a clear definition of success from the previous chapter, you can be proactive in your use of data. Everyone in your school community has to be clear on what the key performance indicators are and where they can find them to determine how students are making progress toward success.

Key performance indicators, or KPIs, are the few, most critical metrics that inform whether or not a goal or objective is accomplished. They are the "at-a-glance" info that provides quick insight as to whether the organization achieves its desired outcomes; they are not spreadsheets of data that contain everything that has been collected at the school. They are not charts and tables that are created to fill pages in a report or slide deck. They are purposeful; they are the *keys* to success.

ATTENTION PLEASE

If your school has any of the following based on your reflections checklist from Part I, this chapter will be important for your work.

- ☐ Lack of agreement about what success indicators are
- ☐ Pressure to meet external accountability standards
- ☐ Limited time for data collection and analysis
- ☐ Faculty or administration without education or training in measurement
- ☐ Reluctance to change classroom practices based on evidence
- ☐ Plans implemented without evaluation practices identified
- ☐ Data Evaders
- ☐ Passive Participants
- ☐ Data Antagonists

The Keys to the Success Kingdom

To build or strengthen the culture around evidence-based decisions, we now turn to E for *exploration*. Here, we address looking at data properly, not ignoring it. When people are not feeling positive about the data or the act of reviewing data, the data journey needs to engage your team differently. With limited time and mixed feelings about data or statistics, it's important to identify and share the KPIs that align to measures of success. What happens if you don't?

During one site visit to an elementary school, all of the teachers gathered to review student results and explore where the strengths and areas of improvement were for the students in their building. This institution was considered a "high-performing" school district and at the forefront of instructional practices as well as data-driven decision-making (a common phrase of the time). They even had their own assessment and accountability team before it was the norm for districts of their size to have in-house staff in these roles.

For the activity I was leading, all of the instructional staff members were invited to review their students' results across the constructs on the assessment. There were five to eight of these skill sets within the test, so we approached the data from three angles:

1. Identify where a skill set was falling short for most of the class; this would lead to a curriculum and instruction discussion,

2. Determine where a skill set was below proficiency for an individual student but not the majority of students in the class; this would inform an opportunity for individual academic intervention, and

3. Review the results to see if some students were strong in some areas but not others or if there were students struggling across multiple areas; this helped to inform the intensity of intervention or indicate a need to focus on foundational skills.

Before getting into the findings, one teacher raised her hand for what I thought was a question. It wasn't. She stood up and said that I was unprofessional.

I felt the rush of heat hit my face. *You said what, now?*

She went on to say how it was unprofessional to be looking at this student information and she was upset at how unprofessional I was. The room full of faculty and administration was silent.

I gathered my thoughts and asked her, "Are these students *your* students? There are no students from other buildings, right?" I knew the answer already, but I wanted to check her understanding of the dataset; other instructors in attendance were flipping through the document[25] and nodding that indeed the students in the report were their students.

I continued to state that we were not violating FERPA[26] since there was a legitimate educational interest in the work being done to support the students sitting in her classroom for whom she was responsible. She had no response to that, and the group proceeded to complete the data activity, making plans for the next steps based on the findings.

After the session, I approached the administration to discuss the follow up needed since they didn't say anything *at all* during the activity or when the teacher challenged my professionalism. The administration meekly apologized for her disruptive behavior with the equivalent of an eye roll, and that was it.

For a high-performing institution, it was clear that the culture of evidence-based decisions was not on solid ground. It was obvious that this Data Antagonist did not have a positive feeling about the data, the act of reviewing data, or the data messenger, probably due to her lack of practice or exposure to using data productively. The activity was something "extra" for her, outside of her comfort zone, and challenged the status quo. The school needed to make the review of data easier, more frequent, and set a professional expectation: all more easily accomplished with KPIs. So what exactly *are* KPIs?

---

25   Yes, I said hard copies. Laptops, tablets, and personal electronic devices were not available at this time.

26   Family educational rights and privacy act (FERPA), August 25, 2021. https://www2.ed.gov/policy/gen/guid/fpco/ferpa/index.html.

KPIs are the most important metrics for making progress toward your goals. Think of the key checkpoints to cross on the way to the final outcome. In the weight loss program example, water intake and grams of sugar consumed may be the most important metrics for me while protein intake and amount of time doing cardio may be the top indicators for someone else. It depends on where each person starts and what the goal is.

Key performance indicators should align to definitions of success and desired outcomes in the short, intermediate, and long term so it's clear what should be tracked and reported. In your school, is reading proficiency a goal? Your strategic plan is probably a five-year plan, so if you want to achieve this goal in five years, where should things be after a year? Three years? What *are* the key checkpoints along the way?

As you implement the plan, it's important to focus on the KPIs that will help move the school from where it is to the long-term outcome. KPIs to track progress toward reading proficiency could be targeted instruction of foundational skills (short term), positive attitudes or engagement in reading (intermediate term), and reading comprehension skills (long term). These will connect back to the success criteria from your team's discussions of what reading achievement means for the students in your institution.

The strategies or actions implemented each year should result in accomplished objectives related to these outcomes. If your school implements activities that address the most important outcomes, then the school should be making progress toward the reading proficiency goal. If a progress check didn't have a review of interim outcomes, then the team is simply exploring at a general level. Is reading comprehension better? Sure, there might be some improvement; however, it may be a result of typical child development, unrelated to the school's efforts. And it's unlikely that there will be enough growth for the students who need the most help. The KPIs will inform the team who needs what support early and keep the team on track toward the end goal.

Once you're clear on the desired outcomes, your school should be tracking progress formally on those KPIs through business intelligence tools or other reporting methods. Many student information systems already have the capacity for building KPI reports; the key is to ensure the reports include the KPIs that matter to *your* institution's goal. And your KPIs are not *APIs* (all performance indicators). They should only be the indicators informing you if you're making progress toward your desired outcomes.

Access to KPIs at all levels of an institution and shared with the public allows the data *exploration* to use the same starting point. Imagine if that disruptive teacher came to the meeting aware of what the KPIs were and understood how her work in the classroom connected to those results. I am sure she would not have made the same public display, and if she did, then the administration would have had a different conversation about her behavior.

Don't Just Admire, Explore!

Now that you have the measures defined and KPIs available, does everyone enjoy the pretty pictures or does your team do something with the information? When a team has access to a lot of well-organized data with minimal use of it, a former colleague of mine called it "admiring the data". We are not running a data museum! How do you cultivate a culture that turns the work from data *appreciation* to data *exploration*?

According to Jim Collins (2001) in *Good to Great*, it is important to confront the brutal facts. Measuring progress doesn't have to be brutal, but a review of the data should include the *climate* he talks about, whereby data can be reviewed and teams can express their thoughts without fear or judgment.

Shifting the culture requires changing the norms around how those responsible for decision-making facilitate data exploration. Let's look to Jim Collins's steps for confronting the brutal facts for help with building that culture:

1. *Lead with questions, not answers,*
2. *Engage in dialogue and debate, not coercion,*

3. *Conduct autopsies, without blame, and*
4. *Build red-flag mechanisms that turn information into information that cannot be ignored.*

Lead with Questions, Not Answers

In a planning session where I worked with an administrative team to review data and identify strengths, weaknesses, opportunities, and threats (SWOT), the school leader said to the team, "Everyone is looking at us for the right answers."

I knew the school was in trouble.

As a school leader, you don't always have the right answers, and that's to be expected. In institutions where stakeholders fail to engage because there is a climate of the leader having the only right answer or where people do not feel their input has value, they won't be able to build a culture around evidence.

To build a culture that embraces evidence, the group needs to trust each other (here we go again with the trust). In his 2019 book, *The Culture Code*, Dan Coyle emphasizes the importance of vulnerability in creating trust. When you are exploring the data, you can engage your team and build trust with questions like:

- *"What am I missing?"*
- *"Can you tell me more about…"*
- *"How could we improve…"*

When you lead with purposeful, open-ended questions about the data, admit that you do not have all of the answers, and value input from all stakeholders, there is a better chance that the data will be explored, not admired. Productive exploration will ensure those Passive Participants and those without formal training in measurement will have an opportunity to contribute.

Engage in Dialogue and Debate, Not Coercion

In one institution where the planning committee identified goals and created KPIs, there were a lot of heated *and* productive discussions. The committee included faculty, administrators, and student representation, and each person approached the review of evidence through their own lens. The goal under scrutiny focused on creating a student experience where all students felt "empowered to succeed." They debated the words in the goal for weeks, consulting the thesaurus, sharing past experiences with the term, and debating how to define "empowerment." Once the goal was set, measuring it was the challenge, particularly because they didn't already have a dashboard with an empowerment-related KPI. It was important for the committee to discuss the construct (using questions from the last chapter) and then review their existing data to determine how they could measure empowerment. The group worked together, discussed and explored, and let the dialogue evolve without pressure or coercion.

Being able to admit they didn't have all the answers, understanding that the data would be used for improvements and not punishments, and agreeing to create a positive experience for students helped them explore the data productively. This approach will also help reduce the disruptions from Data Antagonists.

So, can employees across your institution have a healthy dialogue about defining constructs and reviewing evidence, even if evidence does not support assumptions? Take a minute to reflect on your school data discussions with the following questions:

- *Do staff members feel there will be retaliation if they ask questions about the evidence?*
- *Do they feel that looking at data that do not show the desired results will be used to punish them?*
- *Do they think their input won't matter because a decision or direction was already made before the meeting?*

If any of these answers is yes, then the culture has room for improvement. Set clear expectations for data exploration up front, allow for input from all participants, and lead with questions like those in the last section.

Conduct Autopsies, without Blame

Would we wait until the end of the year and submission of final grades to figure out what course content was giving students the most trouble? If a student fails a class, do we try to figure out what went wrong at the end of the semester, when it is too late to offer help?

Grades should not be a surprise and the results from a strategic plan should not be a surprise, either. It's a given that not everything will go according to the plan. When strategic planning activities are implemented and progress isn't measured regularly, it's easy to get to the end of the planning cycle and question what went wrong. If data haven't been collected, tracked, and discussed throughout the implementation phase, it might be hard or impossible to gather the evidence to understand why the plan didn't lead to desired outcomes. In the absence of evidence, it is easy to lay blame.

When there is a lack of evidence and finger-pointing, it makes staff more likely to avoid engaging in the work moving forward. Remember those Data Evaders? Jim Collins would propose that as the review of what went wrong occurs, there should be a climate that searches for understanding and truth. Instead of exploring data after it's too late to do anything about the situation, your team should look at data like preventative medicine. If you review KPIs frequently and make evidence part of regular activities, then you won't need to conduct an autopsy and wonder "what happened." You and your team will see issues emerge and make necessary pivots before the plan completely dies.

Build Red Flag Mechanisms That Turn Information into Information That Cannot Be Ignored

You are a school leader; you have charisma that helps you work with various groups of people within and outside of the institution. Collins writes,

> If you suffer the liability of charisma, red flag mechanisms give you a practical and useful tool for turning information into information that cannot be ignored and for creating a climate where the truth is heard.

He shared a great example of giving red flags— they were literal red pieces of paper—to students to use once per quarter at any time to stop the class. When they used a red flag, they could say or ask anything, good or bad, related or unrelated. In staff meetings, particularly when there is a history of distrust or if the leader thinks the right answers are expected, this process can open the discussion to all voices. The red flags do not replace other opportunities to contribute; they are designed to allow the meeting, discussion, or activity to stop and listen when someone feels the need to share something.

Try it with your leadership team: one red flag per quarter that is nontransferable to another colleague and doesn't carry into the next quarter if it isn't used. What new insights are generated? How did the team feel about the use of the flags to add to the conversation? Let me know on Facebook or Instagram (*@measureanything*).

Reflection

In this chapter, we turned our definitions of success into the most important evidence that institutions can use to track progress. We recognized when a culture of evidence is absent and what steps you could take to ensure data turn into direction so you can keep the team moving forward toward their goals. With a reinvigorated culture exploring key performance indicators, now we need to focus that energy on the right actions that impact the KPIs.

As a school leader, how are you building a culture that explores evidence? Which of the following are in place and which could be enhanced in the next 6-12 months?		
	In Place	*Needs Improvement*
KPIs are identified and accessible to anyone.		
I lead my team with questions since I do not have all of the answers.		
The leadership team is comfortable engaging in dialogue and debate around evidence.		
The leadership team can review results without assigning blame		
I build feedback mechanisms into team meetings to encourage input from each team member about the most important evidence.		

CHAPTER 6

Changing the Culture— Focus

YOU ARE IN THE SHOWER. YOU THINK YOU SMELL SMOKE. Now the smoke alarm is going off. You run out of the shower, no towels in sight, but you see your outfit laid out on the bed: shirt, jacket, jeans, socks, underwear, hat, belt, and sneakers (okay, the sneakers are on the floor, not on the bed). You only have time to put one thing on. What do you do?

Do you put on your jacket? Hat? Shoes? Do you get overwhelmed with the options and the need to make a quick decision so you leave naked? Do you try to put it all on at once, get tangled in the effort, and die of smoke inhalation?

Clearly, some clothing options are better than others since you might regret leaving the house in only your hat, but if you picked the wrong thing, you would learn from it and make a better plan for the future.

When you don't set a clear direction for a school, it is like you're trying to grab all of your clothes and end up trapped. When you avoid making that choice, it exposes a lack of leadership. Even if your choice isn't the best option, it keeps you alive and better prepared for future decisions. I know it's hard to take a stand about what the school community should focus on; *everything* feels important. However, if you want to make progress toward success and escape stagnation, you can't spread your efforts thin. You must concentrate on one thing.

Let's find your priority in this chapter: F is for *Focus*.

ATTENTION PLEASE

If your school has any of the following based on your reflections checklist from Part I, this chapter will be important for your work.

- ☐ Outdated and/or extremely general mission statement
- ☐ Lack of agreement about what success indicators are
- ☐ Reluctance to change classroom practices based on evidence

But What About...?

Remember our rowing team? For practice and each race, the team is clear about the direction, their roles, and the elements that could impact the success of the task. For them, the endpoint is provided in terms of a finish line, but what is the finish line in your school?

You might think a 100% graduation rate or perhaps 100% placement into the workforce are the finish lines, but I would compare that final result to getting a championship trophy, which is the ultimate goal. There are many finish lines to cross in a season before getting to a championship, and there will be many key checkpoints, such as course completion and retention rates, that an institution looks to en route to a high graduation rate. So do you focus on course completion, retention, and graduation rate at the same time? Which is the most important of the three to focus on first? That is, which is checkpoint A?

Everyone in your school community should be clear on what the priority is. When I work with schools, it can be hard to decide what checkpoint A should be versus checkpoint B, C, or D. Mission statements often have several areas of interest that might make it look like all checkpoints are equally important. So which part of the mission work should come first? With so many distractions competing for your attention on a daily basis piled on top of the school's multi-faceted mission, it can be a challenge to select where to start and identify what is most important to address *today*. As the saying goes, if everything is a priority, nothing is a priority.

In the 2012 Keller and Papasan book, *The ONE Thing*, they discuss the importance of setting a priority—*one priority*—that everyone can focus on. The idea is that you identify the one thing to work on so that by doing so, it makes everything else easy or unnecessary. Like a ripple effect, the one thing that becomes your focus can have a positive impact on other issues. For example, focusing on engaging instruction will impact disruptive behaviors.

It's important that once you set the focus, you stick with it for a while and see the impact it has in your school. In my career, I've seen schools jump on the latest trend, such as a math program or behavior intervention. Soon after implementation, before it has a chance to succeed, they abandon the project due to lack of results (and then wonder why nothing they try ever works). In their 2011 book, *Great by Choice*, Collins and Hansen share a story about a "Beat the Odds" school in Arizona that saw desired outcomes because they didn't abandon their efforts too early. The team implemented instructional strategies to improve reading skills, explored data, adjusted instruction, provided individual student interventions, and *gave the program time to work*. Collins called this "fanatic discipline" on one focused goal. The staff remained focused on their goal to increase basic skills in reading, and it made a substantial difference[27].

So the idea of focus isn't new, but it can be a challenge to find the focus and stay focused. This challenge reminds me of an old *Seinfeld* episode where Jerry makes a car rental reservation after his car was stolen. He makes a reservation for a mid-size car, and the agent tells him they ran out of mid-size cars. Perplexed and frustrated, Jerry comments that the agent could "take the reservation" but didn't know how to "hold the reservation." He goes on to say that the "hold" is the most important part of the reservation and that anyone could take a reservation. There was humor in the scene; however, when this scenario plays out in schools that can *find* a focus but can't *hold* their focus, it hurts students and frustrates staff and taxpayers. Any leader can create a goal or set a priority, but it is more important to hold that focus and execute actions that align with your goal.

What keeps school leaders from finding and keeping a focus?

27   Jim Collins and Morten Hansen, "20 Mile March – Building Confidence in K12 Education," accessed August 15, 2024, https://www.jimcollins.com/article_topics/articles/20-mile-march.html#articletop.

1. They are afraid to focus
(a.k.a. The Case of the What Abouts).

How do teams react when they are asked to focus on one thing? In my experience, they're concerned that others will think they aren't doing enough. For those concerned that the general public will think that, usually the discussion is peppered with "what abouts." If we are all focused on communication, then what about instruction? What about safety? What about assessment?

In these situations, the "what abouts" are generally related to the day-to-day operations, not a strategic, purposeful activity to move the lever toward success. Schools will always need to teach, be safe, and assess progress, but how are you communicating about it in a way that engages parents? How do faculty across buildings communicate what is working for students and what needs to change? How are instructional staff communicating with students about the progress they are making? How are students able to share their voices if they do not feel safe? Communication can be the priority *and* improve other areas of operations.

2. They think multitasking is productive (and it's not).

There is plenty of research about the downside of multitasking: it makes us *less* productive, not more productive.[28] Schools know this is true deep down. I remember sitting in on regional scoring of state tests, and the evaluation of rubric-based items was done to minimize task-switching. That is, the scorers were to evaluate all item one responses across all students first before moving on to question two. This prevented a mental recalibration for each item. If they tried to go back and forth between the items for each test, the amount of time to complete the task would increase, and fatigue would set in sooner, leading to more errors in their work.

While much of the multitasking research focuses on the impact on an individual's productivity, I see similar productivity killers at an

---

28   "Multitasking: Switching Costs." American Psychological Association, accessed August 15, 202, https://www.apa.org/topics/research/multitasking.

institutional level. When schools have multiple priorities (usually seen as several different goals in their strategic plan), they continually recalibrate their time, energy, and resources. Often they spread themselves thin and tasks get delayed or ignored. I worked with several schools that had more than one focus area in their strategic plan. When it came time to measure progress, they realized that their split focus impeded progress across the board. How could they prepare students for post-secondary pursuits AND strengthen communication AND revamp their instructional strategies all at the same time? By resetting their attention to one thing—one priority to start with—the teams were better able to collaborate, maximize resources, and achieve success.

3. They are overwhelmed with inputs, often experiencing decision fatigue.

Think back to our shower example. If it is too hard to choose an item and you leave the house au naturel, you've hit decision fatigue. With so many decisions you have to make every day and so many data points coming at you from every direction, how can you decide what is most important?

In interviews I conduct for administrative assistants, I include a prioritization task. The candidate is given index cards with five tasks that are typically encountered in a day. For example, the five tasks might be: sending an invoice, calling back an existing client, calling back a potential client, responding to a request for payment, and posting about an upcoming event on social media. All tasks need to get done; however, I ask the candidate to put them in order and explain why the choices were made.

This activity provides insight into how someone understands the tasks required of the position and how they identify what's important. If the candidate says, "I would just get them all done," that is the same as you telling your school community you have a strategic plan with four goals and twenty objectives that will be done in the next five years. Just like I wouldn't be confident with the candidate who would "just get it all done," your school community is likely to be skeptical about your chances of success without a clear focus.

4. Distractions get prioritized.

An open door policy in your office is nice. It shows you are available and approachable. The person stopping by feels important and heard. The distraction becomes the priority as you are taken away from what you were doing. But what happens when you are interrupted all day long?

When you don't have a clear priority to focus on, every distraction gets attention that keeps you from accomplishing what you set out to achieve. A clear priority helps to *keep* focus so that other distractions, trends, or random ideas don't derail progress. The focus becomes the lens by which all aspects of the institution can be strengthened. With the singular focus, you aren't necessarily doing new things; rather, you are doing things with a new purpose and building a unified strategy to make things better.

Found Focus

When you can move through the obstacles keeping you from finding your focus, it will get your team energized, coordinated, and committed. In one institution my team and I worked with, there were a number of barriers left over from past planning efforts, such as too many goals, lack of shared vision, and performance gaps. Under new leadership, Onondaga Community College had to refocus. My team and I were charged with identifying needs and helping to develop a five-year strategy related to new student enrollment, student success (retention, persistence, and graduation), social justice, and management and care of resources. That's a lot to focus on! After my team and I conducted a needs assessment and reviewed key themes and recommendations from stakeholders, it was clear that the priority for the next strategic plan needed to be *persistence*.

Persistence is the term for the desire to continue to achieve goals in spite of challenges that come their way. Hearing various perspectives and reviewing SWOT[29] information for the college (the process is described in the next section), the decision was that persistence was the one thing that, by focusing on it, would make other areas easier or

29   Strengths/Weaknesses/Opportunities/Threats

unnecessary to change. That means if the school could get students to complete courses and re-enroll for the next semester (persistence) by removing barriers, there was a better chance they'd continue to the next year (retention), and ultimately graduate.

The construct of *persistence* was further explored through three pillars: *academic success, student experience,* and *communication.* Goals and key performance indicators were created and aligned to the three pillars *with a consistent focus on improving persistence.* So as programs and services are being shaped and implemented under this strategic plan, the question becomes, how will these efforts help students complete their coursework and have a positive experience so they will enroll in another semester?

Finding Your Focus

How do you get focused on "the *one* thing" your team needs to pay attention to when there are so many things thrown at you every day? I find the classic SWOT analysis helps move the team from data to direction, from fragmented to focused. We briefly mentioned SWOT in the last chapter, so let's go over how to do it to get that clear direction.

SWOT stands for strengths, weaknesses, opportunities, and threats and is used a lot for strategic planning in all sectors. Strengths and weaknesses are *internal* to the institution and opportunities and threats are *external.* In developing a future focus, the aim is to maximize strengths and opportunities and minimize weaknesses and threats. Remember in Part I when we talked about reducing error? It's the same idea here. We want to tamp down anything that will impede the school's ability to be successful.

In education, the findings of a comprehensive needs assessment or environmental scan[30] provide a foundation from which to extract the strengths, weaknesses, opportunities, and threats. This is a critical step so the team is exploring and using evidence, not opinions or personal interests, to shape the future of the institution.

---

30   We conduct comprehensive needs assessments by collecting data from all stakeholders, reviewing documents and existing data, and other pertinent information as needed;
some refer to this as an environmental scan.

How to SWOT Your School

When conducting SWOT activities over the years, my team and I have asked leadership teams, strategic planning committees, and boards of education to review the results of their needs assessments, and then identify three to five strengths, weaknesses, opportunities, and threats using the SWOT Template below. The SWOT Template is also available as a downloadable worksheet at *www.yourschoolsucks.com/resources*.

SWOT TEMPLATE

	Positive	Negative
Internal	strengths	weaknesses
External	opportunities	threats

Strengths and weaknesses are considered to be "internal" or under the purview of the institution; that is, within their sphere of influence or control. The opportunities and threats are "external" to the institution. They might be known, or they could be a surprise. The COVID-19 pandemic was an unknown threat at first. Now schools are more aware that health crises or other threats could require them to shut down operations or change modalities quickly.

For **strengths**, what exists *within* the institution that stakeholders identify as a top positive quality? What helps lift the institution toward greater success?

For **weaknesses**, what do stakeholders identify as a limitation, obstacle, or challenge that exists *within* the institution? What gets in the way of progress?

For **opportunities**, what exists *outside* of an institution that could assist the institution in achieving its goals? These are resources, partnerships, funding streams or anything external to the institution that can accelerate progress.

For **threats**, what exists *outside* of the institution that could hinder progress? What external mandates, pressures, challenges are going to present obstacles that could lead the institution to focus energy or resources away from the priority?

Once three to five items are added per quadrant and the group has a chance to compile all input, my team and I ask the participants to refine the group feedback and identify the top S, W, O, and T. Was there a consensus among the group? If there were differences, what evidence in the needs assessment led to differing viewpoints? This open communication also models the elements of confronting the brutal facts outlined in the last chapter.

Guiding Question to Set the Priority

Once the top S, W, O, and T are clarified, we ask: *what is the* one *thing the school community should focus on over the next five years to get closer to the school's mission?* The priority should minimize W and T while leveraging S and O. By focusing on one priority and putting the first thing first, it will make other concerns easier or unnecessary to work on, thereby saving time, energy, and shrinking resources.

SAMPLE SWOT SUMMARY

	Positive	Negative
Internal	strengths	weaknesses
	• Consistent leadership (10)* • Small size (8) • Extracurriculars (6) • Teachers care about students (5) • Lots of professional development (4)	• Communication/PR (10) • Disengaged teachers (7) • Increasing absenteeism (staff and students) (7) • Small size (6)
External	opportunities	threats
	• Local YMCA and library have educational programs (8) • Grant writer (5) • Partnerships with other schools (5) • New Chamber of Commerce leadership (3)	• Reduced state funding (10) • No public transportation (8) • Lack of preschool options in the community (6)

Numbers in Parentheses Represent Number of Participants Noting That Item

Based on this SWOT Summary, the school chose to address two areas: 1) communications, focusing on accuracy and consistency of message and sharing a variety of voices, and 2) staff and student engagement through career connections. Central Office Administration took the lead on the communications priority which was more operational in nature; they already communicate, they just need to do it better. Building Leadership Teams focused on strategic engagement, meaning it would help advance the institution's mission the most. With the engagement focus important for making progress, it would be highlighted frequently in communications about the institution. With a singular strategic focus, the school was able to organize its monetary, time, and human resources most effectively.

Root Causes

Some might look at the priority area as the "root cause" of the concerns in a school. In my experience, I find the more you seek a root cause, the more the team tends to shift from an internal focus to an external focus. That is, in seeking a cause for a problem, it is easy to blame factors outside of the school's control. For example, when searching for why parents aren't engaged, it is easy for the root cause conversation to jump from lack of effective school communications to parents not valuing education. For those who point toward external factors as the root cause instead of threats that need to be minimized in strategy work, it could derail school transformation efforts.

As a facilitator, when I get to the point where external factors are emphasized in an attempt to end the session, I need to explore beyond that using a *why* and *how* activity. Instead of going into more *why*s in a root cause analysis (e.g., *why* do parents not care? They didn't have a good school experience. *Why* didn't they have a good school experience? And the dig continues…), we stop asking why after a few rounds and switch to a *how* question. *How* can the school help parents care more? Usually it leads to things that the school *can* impact, such as improvement in outreach efforts in this engagement example. And those *how* answers connect back to the *one* thing the school can focus on.

Reflection

A shared focus—or priority—for your institution is necessary to achieve the levels of success you desire for your students and school community. The priority should be based on stakeholder needs and drive the direction of strategic initiatives. This focus is chosen as the entry point, the first domino, that will make progress toward desired outcomes. And when you get past checkpoint A, it may make other strategic initiatives easier or even unnecessary to address in the long run.

The institutional priority will change over time as progress is made and new needs are identified. This should be part of the process and scheduled in the planning cycle, not changed based on a whim or a new leader's latest pet project.

In the past few chapters, we have been talking about D, E, and F as separate components, so what does it look like in an institution that has done all three? And does the order matter? Go ahead and complete the reflection checklist below and then take a look at the DEF combinations in the next chapter.

As a school leader, how are you currently identifying the one *most important focus? What should you include in your planning efforts in the next six to twelve months?*

- ☐ *Needs assessments are used to identify S, W, O, T.*
- ☐ *Various stakeholders provide input regarding the priority area.*
- ☐ *The strategic plan is built with a singular area of focus.*
- ☐ *Goals and KPIs are designed with the priority area in mind.*

CHAPTER 7

Putting DEF
Into Practice

"Three is the magic number."
Schoolhouse Rock

IMAGINE WHAT KIND OF SUCCESS *YOUR* SCHOOL COULD realize with DEF seamlessly functioning. Collaborative **discussions** that define success criteria, **exploration** of key performance indicators that measure success criteria, and a clear **focus** about how to achieve your goals. Sounds like a dream come true or like some type of magic, but it isn't magic. It's the formula for success where you are setting up systems to reduce the error that keeps success out of reach. With your leadership and the DEF approach, you can make the image of your school's future a reality.

Throughout this chapter, we will provide some ideas to make the ideal future more concrete by reviewing what DEF looks like when done in different sequences. You will also find a case study of one specific institution that has implemented DEF approaches to great success. The institution's journey wasn't smooth or perfectly linear; however, the team stayed the course using the DEF approach. It's exciting to see the progress when DEF comes together, especially knowing that it can be done in your institution too.

For each of the following reordered DEF scenarios, consider which sounds most like your institution. Where is your starting point? Are there pieces of the puzzle missing or perhaps not fully developed?

F–E–D

When schools have just F and E, they have a focus area, like student behavior or chronic absenteeism, and may have data regarding suspensions, expulsions, and attendance. To make progress toward improving behavior, the leadership team needs to clarify what it looks like when student behavior or absenteeism is at its best. When the success criteria are identified, it might require a new focus on different data elements.

For example, in one school I worked with, there was a concern with chronic absenteeism, and we needed to know why and what the school would look like if the problem was fixed. The team suggested that the school would be full of students who wanted to be there, they looked forward to going to class, and the parents would make sure students got to school (not every child was bussed). Aha! Now we are looking at an engagement issue. A new focus was warranted, and KPIs were needed to track engagement as well as attendance data.

E–F–D

In this sequence, an institution decides to collect information about stakeholder needs and other student outcomes. Perhaps they see some performance gaps and then choose what to focus on. Finally, they identify success criteria based on the area of focus.

For example, in one institution, the data revealed performance gaps in underrepresented minority populations. There was an interest in addressing that gap as a focus in the planning efforts. This is where I came into the conversation. There were some discussions about what success would look like; however, this sequence did not yield enough information to determine *how* the school should work to close the performance gap. The school then collected more data about student perceptions, established success criteria based on those findings, and then set a focus (yes, the sequence shifted to E-D-F) on aspects of the student experience which led to a more actionable plan.

F–D–E

In this order, the institution identifies a focus, discusses the desired outcomes, and then explores data for the baseline and growth. This is a common sequence when the school leader inherits a plan from someone else. The priority is set, the results are expected, and then things start happening. When exploration comes after the implementation of strategies, the school tends to commit to too many actions (similar to the concept of throwing spaghetti against the wall to see what sticks), and resources might be spent on the wrong things.

For example, I've seen a school focus on culture and discuss the desire to have everyone respected and feeling safe. The school hired culture experts and a social worker, and invested in more extracurricular opportunities. However, disruptive behaviors continued, staff morale declined, and students weren't participating in extracurriculars as much. This is where I came in to help collect data to determine what the culture issues were and for whom. With this new evidence, the school reset its cultural focus by defining success as a sense of belonging (for staff and students). This focus combined with clear KPIs allowed the team to implement the right strategies for the right people.

D–F–E

For this sequence, the institution may already have a focus based on discussions of what success means for the school. However, the leadership team may have used opinions and personal experiences instead of an exploration of data to set the direction. As the school prepares to implement a set of actions to address the priority, the institution then collects and explores data.

Similar to the last scenario, this approach usually requires a reset of focus and success criteria once data are collected and explored. My team and I have worked with this type of institution, and as I mentioned at the beginning of Part II, without data, there's frustration with the plan when it's built on a limited set of leadership perspectives. And this is when we come in to help the team get unstuck. Exploring data and gathering input from multiple perspectives ensures everyone is working toward the same outcome. Once E enters the process, the school gains new momentum as the plan is fine-tuned based on evidence.

Case Study: E-D-F then D-E-F

The following case study chronicles two strategic planning cycles with two different DEF sequences. Located in the Southern Tier of New York, Hornell City School District (CSD) experienced a change in district leadership in 2017. The new superintendent, Jeremy Palotti, acknowledged that there were shared areas of interest and intentions to make improvements, but there was little evidence of continuity on a district level. During the first five-year planning cycle, the work progressed from **exploration** to **discussion** to **focus** (E-D-F). Here is part one of the story.

As noted earlier, when exploration comes first, an institution decides that before it can define success criteria, it needs to collect information about stakeholder needs and other student outcomes. My team and I used a research-based framework to guide survey, interview, and focus group protocols; the framework was built upon multiple constructs that served as key metrics of interest. Constructs like effective leadership and a supportive learning environment were utilized to organize the evidence. Data from stakeholder groups and information from current district plans, accountability reports, and other relevant documents were reviewed to inform actionable findings for each construct.

Then, the team discussed what success would look like based on the identified needs. My team and I facilitated discussions with Hornell CSD Board of Education members and administrators to create short-term, intermediate-term, and long-term desired outcomes based on evidence, not opinions.

After that, the leadership team set the priority or focus to achieve the desired results. Addressing the areas that would impact the instructional program outcomes the most, Alla Breve Consulting worked with leadership teams to create building-level goals and action plans, including processes to evaluate the attainment of the goals. This E-D-F sequence is one that my team and I typically follow when there is a need to create a new strategic plan.

As a result of the work facilitated by Alla Breve Consulting, Hornell CSD secured a $1.57 million Innovative Approaches to Literacy grant from the U.S. Department of Education (USDOE). Literacy strategies that were a priority in K-6 now had additional resources for effective implementation starting in grades pre-K through three.

With continued measurement of progress, in 2021, the District secured an additional $3 million literacy grant from the USDOE. The funds were focused on expanding literacy programs and services for students in the Intermediate School, providing continuity and consistency through sixth grade.

In sum, Hornell CSD conducted a needs assessment and *explored* evidence to determine the areas in need of strengthening. And then through *discussion* of the findings, they defined what outcomes they wanted to achieve. Finally, the leadership team determined that consistency of curriculum should be the pre-K through sixth grade *focus*, specifically looking at literacy as a gatekeeper to other academic areas.

Part two of the story began in 2022 when Hornell CSD started a new needs assessment and strategic planning process; however, the sequence of events shifted to **discussion**, then **exploration**, and then **focus** (D-E-F). The second cycle built off of the success realized in the prior five years and identified a revised focus based on the current needs of constituents. The team discussed what was accomplished and what was still to be done in other areas like supportive learning environments and post-secondary preparation. With those outcomes not entirely achieved, they served as the foundation for the next round of planning. Data were explored with attention on the learning environment and revealed the need to focus on stronger mental health systems and improved collaboration across family, community, and school partners. In round two, the leadership team saw the need for fewer goals and a more narrow focus for their planning efforts so they could coordinate resources and achieve more.

According to Superintendent Palotti,

> the district stakeholders needed to be fully engaged at the ground level with voices being heard along the way. Upon reflecting on the process and results, I have come to see that this process is just what Hornell needed.

Through discussions across stakeholders about what success is for the students it serves, exploration of data (not just easy to collect information), and identification of a priority or shared focus, Hornell CSD continues to reinforce a solid foundation, making measurable progress both *with their* and *for their* constituents.

Summing It Up

So in your school, they don't have to be done in order, but they *all* need to be incorporated into your institution's culture to achieve the desired levels of success.

In short:

Discussion: come to a consensus about the definition of the constructs and desired outcomes so you can measure them.

Exploration: measure and track the key performance indicators that align to the desired outcomes.

Focus: identify a single priority that will guide actions to achieve desired results.

How can you strengthen this work with your own institution? Remember three is the magic number; the order depends on where you are starting. If you haven't started this work yet or it has been a while, E-D-F could be the best entry point.

Conclusion

"I have never let schooling interfere with my education."
GRANT ALLEN (although often attributed to Mark Twain)

EVEN AS FAR BACK AS THE LATE 1800S, PEOPLE THOUGHT school sucked. Grant Allen's quote implies that school settings do not further, but rather can interfere with, one's education. I think it is time to change that idea. Through your leadership and the DEFs of this book, it can.

The purpose of this book is to help you get your school community clear on what success means, learn how to create systems to use evidence to drive direction, and find your focus. With your leadership and lessons from this book, you can ensure that errors in decision-making are minimized, there is consensus about direction, and there is momentum toward the success you want to achieve.

Byron-Bergen Central School District is a great example of building momentum. With the help of my team, the district explored evidence through a needs assessment and discovered that a small district can be impacted significantly by seemingly minor situations—whether positive or negative. They knew they had to work together as a unified front to reduce negative situations and improve the instructional environment. Once the building teams drafted initial action plans, the district identified a theme for their five-year strategic plan: *Many Bees, One Hive.* This theme supported the emphasis on building an engaging, differentiated, rigorous learning environment where multiple perspectives are valued so students can achieve their highest potential.

The theme of *Many Bees, One Hive* serves as a reminder of the central priority, and this declaration of unity can be found on internal and external communications and signage in each building. According to Patrick McGee, Superintendent of Schools,

> I knew we needed a blueprint for success. What really set this approach apart from others was the work the Alla Breve team did with our stakeholders, including our building and district-level teams. Their facilitation helped with buy-in and the mindset that we *all* own this plan. Our *Many Bees, One Hive* theme for the plan has created a lot of momentum, with a clear and shared focus for the district.

When an institution isn't clear on how to get to that desired outcome, doesn't measure progress, or lacks a shared focus, it is sure to get off course. When your school veers off course, it costs time and resources. The more delays and detours, the more you spend and longer it takes to get things done.

I challenge you to reflect with your teams, your schools, and your friends and colleagues—what does success mean for the students and communities you serve today? What is the best course of action, the priority, for your students today to ensure you can attain the levels of success you want to see a year, two years, or even five years from now?

The final reflection questions to ask are:

- *Discussion:* Do you have consensus about the definition of the constructs and desired outcomes that matter most to your institution?
- *Exploration:* Do you have a way to measure and track the key performance indicators that align to your desired outcomes?
- *Focus:* Do you have a clear, shared priority identified and communicated throughout your school community?

I know how hard faculty and staff work and how much you and your leadership team care about the success of your students. What I'd like to see in education as a result of changing perceptions and practices around evidence-based decision-making is a unified vision about what success means for *your* students in *your* institution.

Through discussions, exploration, and shared focus, not only will your school be better at defining and measuring success, it will be better at achieving it.

As we wrap up, here are a few action steps to help you get started or strengthen your leadership:

• *Implement DEF in your institution.*

Most of what you read in this book doesn't require doing something completely new; it requires doing something purposeful. A good place to start is to get clear on success criteria for your institution's most important construct. Using the questions provided in the "Discussion" chapter, make sure your definitions are clear about what the outputs and outcomes are and what evidence is needed to show success.

If the use of evidence to drive decisions is limited or absent, then evaluate how well your leadership team confronts the brutal facts. What can you implement to ensure key performance indicators are known, discussed, and used to track progress?

Need assistance with any of this? That is where my company, Alla Breve Consulting, comes in. Send an email to hello@allabreveconsulting.com with the subject line, "Let's Get Started" and we can set up a call to discuss your situation.

• *Check out our website for more resources, to book a consultation, or just stay connected.*

Not sure where to start? Encountering obstacles during implementation? Don't go it alone. Visit our website at www.yourschoolsucks.com/resources to explore PDFs and other resources related to the content in this book, to book a consultation with our team, or join our Measure Up Mastermind. You can also sign up for our email newsletter, "Measure Up," for more tips and stories to guide your journey.

• Subscribe to our podcast for more ideas and strategies to strengthen your evidence-based culture.

Did you light up when we mentioned collecting evidence? Does someone at your institution love conducting research and measuring progress? Are you curious how others define constructs and measure things that are hard to define? Subscribe to our podcast, *You Can Measure Anything* ®, to build your methodology muscle. We have interviews with experts across many fields who are measuring hard to clarify constructs, ideas for how to measure what matters, and suggestions that help you support best practices. Listen to the podcast at www.youcanmeasure-anything.com or on your favorite podcast platform.

• Share this book with people who can help you execute these ideas.

The school community can be powerful when resources and efforts are coordinated. Share this book with your team and colleagues who also want to see more success and make a bigger impact for the students and communities they serve. Throughout the book we talked about the importance of rowing in the same direction, communicating key metrics, and sharing a singular focus: they all require collaboration.

And remember, I'm here if you need me to ensure no one ever thinks your school sucks.

Acknowledgments

THERE ARE MANY PEOPLE WHO HAVE INSPIRED OR encouraged this book over the decades it has been percolating in my brain.

First, thanks to the TEDxNortheasternU team for allowing me to present my "idea worth spreading" (and an idea that could change everything[31]), "Measuring Success for Better Schools,"[32] and for forcing me to cut out enough from my talk to realize that I needed to find a way to put it all back in! Also, thanks to Lisa Powell Graham for helping me clarify the idea and solidify my voice in the conversation about measurement in education.

Next, thanks to the Alla Breve Consulting team—past, present, and future—for being part of the journey, asking great questions, and supporting clients in this important work. And thanks to the institutions I have had the privilege to assist, with special thanks to those who allowed me to share their success stories.

A huge thanks goes out to Madison Fitzpatrick for getting my decades of experience organized and providing accountability to get this book done. And thanks to Nicole Jobe and her team for getting this project across the finish line.

Lastly, thanks to Paul, Natasha, and all of the "Lab Assistants." You inspire me to make a difference every day.

---

31   TED rebranded with a new tagline "Ideas Change Everything" during the writing of this book.

32   Watch at *www.yourschoolsucks.com/resources*

References

Asch, S. E. "Effects of group pressure upon the modification and distortion of judgments". In *Groups, leadership and men; research in human relations*, edited by H. Guetzkow. Pittsburgh: Carnegie Press, 1951.

Bernard, Sara. "Science Shows Making Lessons Relevant Really Matters." Edutopia, December 1, 2010. https://www.edutopia.org/neuroscience-brain-based-learning-relevance-improves-engagement.

Bigdata. "50+ Incredible Big Data Statistics for 2024: Facts, Market Size & Industry Growth." Big Data Analytics News, March 1, 2024. https://bigdataanalyticsnews.com/big-data-statistics/#:~:text=The%20global%20big%20data%20technology,13.6%25%20during%20the%20forecast%20period.

"Reading Performance." U.S. Department of Education, Institute of Education Sciences. Accessed April 13, 2024. https://nces.ed.gov/programs/coe/indicator/cnb?tid=4.

Collins, Jim. *Good to Great: Why Some Companies Make the Leap ... and Others Don't.* New York: HarperCollins, 2001.

Collins, Jim, and Morton T. Hansen. *Great by Choice: Uncertainty, Chaos, and Luck—Why Some Thrive Despite Them All.* New York: HarperCollins, 2011.

Covey, Stephen R. *The Seven Habits of Highly Effective People: Restoring the Character Ethic.* New York: Simon and Schuster, 1989.

Cunningham, Keith J. *The Road Less Stupid: Advice from the Chairman of the Board*. N.p.: Keys to the Vault, 2017.

Cherones, T., dir. *Seinfeld*. Season 3, episode 11, "The Alternate Side." Aired December 4, 1991, on NBC.

Dollard, John, Neal E. Miller, Leonard W. Doob, O. H. Mowrer, and Robert R. Sears. *Frustration and Aggression*. New Haven, CT: Yale University Press, 1939.

Family Educational Rights and Privacy Act (FERPA). 20 U.S.C. § 1232g. https://www2.ed.gov/policy/gen/guid/fpco/ferpa/index.html.

Hooper, T., dir. *Poltergeist*. Metro-Goldwyn-Mayer, SLM Production Group, Mist Entertainment, Amblin Productions, MGM/UA Entertainment Co., 1982.

Pollock, Jane E. "How Feedback Leads to Engagement." ASCD, https://www.ascd.org/el/articles/how-feedback-leads-to-engagement.

Hughes, J., dir. *Ferris Bueller's Day Off*. Paramount Pictures, 1986.

Nobel, Carmen. "How to Spot a Liar." HBS Working Knowledge. May 13, 2013. https://hbswk.hbs.edu/item/how-to-spot-a-liar.

Johnson, B., L. Martinez-Berman, and C. Curley. "Formation of Attitudes: How People (Wittingly or Unwittingly) Develop Their Viewpoints." *Oxford Research Encyclopedia of Psychology*, edited by Oliver Braddock. Oxford University Press, 2014.

Keller, Gary, and Jay Papasan. *The ONE Thing: The Surprisingly Simple Truth Behind Extraordinary Results*. Austin, TX: Bard Press, 2012.

"Multitasking: Switching costs." American Psychological Association. March 20, 2006. https://www.apa.org/topics/research/multitasking

Ken O'Connor. *A Repair Kit for Grading: 15 Fixes for Broken Grades.* Portland, OR: Educational Testing Service, 2007.

Schachter, Stanley. *The Psychology of Affiliation: Experimental Studies of the Sources of Gregariousness.* Stanford, CA: Stanford University Press, 1974.

Smith, Tim. "What Is Employee Engagement? Definition, Strategies, and Example." Investopedia. https://www.investopedia.com/terms/e/employee-engagement.asp.

Spottiswoode, R., dir. *And the Band Played On.* Spelling Entertainment, HBO Pictures, 1993.

Stevens, S.S."The operational definition of psychological concepts." Psychological Review, vol. 42, no. 6 (1935): 517–527. https://doi.org/10.1037/h0056973.

"What Is Psychometrics?". Psychometric Society. https://www.psychometricsociety.org/what-psychometrics#:~:text=Psychometrics%20is%20a%20scientific%20discipline,attributes%20(e.g.%2C%20intelligence).

www.ingramcontent.com/pod-product-compliance
Lightning Source LLC
Chambersburg PA
CBHW060246030426
42335CB00014B/1612